19 MILES
CAMBODIA 1970
and Other Stories

John S. Tomko, Jr.

outskirts
press

19 Miles
Cambodia 1970 and Other Stories
All Rights Reserved.
Copyright © 2022 John S. Tomko, Jr.
v5.0

The opinions expressed in this manuscript are solely the opinions of the author and do not represent the opinions or thoughts of the publisher. The author has represented and warranted full ownership and/or legal right to publish all the materials in this book.

This book may not be reproduced, transmitted, or stored in whole or in part by any means, including graphic, electronic, or mechanical without the express written consent of the publisher except in the case of brief quotations embodied in critical articles and reviews.

Outskirts Press, Inc.
http://www.outskirtspress.com

ISBN: 978-1-9772-5229-6

Cover Design by Chase Nickoles & Interior Images by John S. Tomko, Jr. © 2022 All rights reserved - used with permission.

Outskirts Press and the "OP" logo are trademarks belonging to Outskirts Press, Inc.

PRINTED IN THE UNITED STATES OF AMERICA

Table of Contents

PREFACE i
PART 1 OPENING SALVO 1
PART 2 THE BEGINNING – 1968 3
PART 3 SOUTH VIETNAM – 1970 18
    Cam Ranh Bay 18
    Camp Frenzell-Jones 19
    FSB Gladys 22
    Wildlife 25
    Another Day in a Grunt's Life 26
    "Sir, This Isn't a Mech Company." 29
    It's Heavy, and It Kicks Ass! 30
    Not Tin Soldiers and Nixon 31
    Extraction (Not the Dental Kind) 32
    Anticipation and Anxiety 32
PART 4 CAMBODIA May-June 1970 35
    MAY 1, 1970 – THE CAMBODIA INCURSION 35
    Phouc Binh (Song Be) 36
    USO, "Georgie Who?" 40
    Payback 41
    Crazy and Just Plain Stupid – May 24, 1970 42
    June 11-12 2000 Bicycles and Other Treasures 44
    Combat Is Horrible, Awful and a Nightmare, June 16-22 .. 46
PART 5 SOUTH VIETNAM, AGAIN 58
PART 6 THE WORLD – 1971 65
EPILOGUE 70
AFTERWORD 74
ACKNOWLEDGMENTS 77

A warrior knows each battle is a dress rehearsal for a final act not yet scripted. He knows each battle may be his last and he wants his last act on this earth to be his finest. If he dies his final story will be told by his brothers and he wants his last account to be one of dignity, honor and duty. A warrior accepts the fact he will either die in battle or resume the life of an average man after his war and the longer he survives the more he will wonder is there a difference. Living and existing are sometimes confused for the same in the civilized world but warriors learn they are not associated. It is difficult to relish life unless you have called death's bluff and the lion's share of warriors have done so. They have seen Death's handiwork and heard his seductive voice beckoning in the distance. Life is cheap but living is priceless.

Sergeant Lloyd Cates
D Company 5th Battalion 12th Infantry
199th Infantry Brigade (Light)
Vietnam July 1969 to July 1970
Over 50 Years of Redcatchers 199th Infantry Brigade
Viet Nam 1966 - 1970

PREFACE

IN 1945, FOLLOWING Japanese occupation during World War II, modern Vietnam was created when Vietnam declared its independence from France. Between 1945 and 1954, during the First Indochina War, France failed to regain its colonies. In May 1954, Viet Minh communist revolutionaries under General Vo-Nguyen Giap decisively defeated the French Far East Expeditionary Corps at Dien Bien Phu. The 1954 Geneva Accords divided the country at the 17th parallel. The north became the Democratic Republic of Vietnam and the south the State of Vietnam, later named the Republic of Vietnam.

During this same period, there was turmoil in Cambodia. Norodom Sihanouk pre-empted an overthrow of Cambodia by the Democratic Republic of Vietnam and the Worker's Party of Vietnam by allowing the Ho Chi Minh Trail to run through the country's eastern provinces. With terminus points for the Ho Chi Minh Trail, both the Parrot's Beak and Fishhook salients of Cambodia played an important role in the Vietnam War in 1970.

Since 1950, the United States had been supporting the French and then the South Vietnamese. In 1959, US troop strength in the Republic of Vietnam was 760, with the US Army in a predominantly advisory role. In July 1959, two American Military Assistance Advisory Group (MAAG) advisors, Major Dale Buis (Panel 1E, Line 1) and Master Sergeant Chester Ovnand (Panel 7E, Line 46), were the first casualties in the Vietnam War (Second Indochina War).

Between August 1964 and March 1973, approximately 1,736,000

US Army soldiers served in Vietnam. In January 1970, the US Army strength in the Republic of Vietnam was 330,300. Operation KEYSTONE BLUEJAY at the end of the month accounted for the redeployment of 50,000 US personnel from the theater of operations. And between July 1 and December 31, Operation KEYSTONE ROBIN brought Army strength to 57,000 with the departure of the 199th Infantry Brigade (Light), the 3rd Brigade 9th Infantry Division, the 1st and 2nd Brigades 4th Infantry Division and the 1st and 3rd Brigades 25th Infantry Division. In 1973 the US troop level was 50. The US Army's role in the Republic of Vietnam officially ended in March. During the war, 25% (648,500) of the total forces in Vietnam were draftees and they accounted for 30.4% (17,725) of the combat deaths. On January 27, 1973, Colonel William Nolde (Panel W1 Line 112) was killed in **An Loc** and was the last official US casualty. The war ended in 1975. The once non-communist south united with the communist north to form the Socialist Republic of Vietnam. **Saigon** became **Ho Chi Minh City.**

The 199th Infantry Brigade (Light) was activated at Fort Benning, Georgia, on June 1, 1966. Its role was counterinsurgency with an emphasis on mobility. The three UH-1 Huey helicopters in the upper center of this book's cover represent this mobility. The Brigade's mission was to seek out and destroy communist cadres in the Republic of Vietnam. Hence the nickname "Redcatchers." In January 1967, after intensive stateside training, the Brigade deployed to the Republic of Vietnam. It operated in the III Corps Tactical Zone under the control of II Field Force in and around **Long Binh** north of **Saigon**. The Brigade spent forty-six months in country.

The 199th Infantry Brigade (Light) was composed of a Headquarters and Headquarters Company and four infantry battalions: the 2nd Battalion 3rd Infantry, the 3rd Battalion 7th Infantry, and the 4th and 5th Battalions of the 12th Infantry. Additional units comprised the combat service and combat service support elements of the Brigade. These were the 2nd Battalion 40th Artillery (Towed), Troop D 17th Cavalry (Armored), the 87th Engineer Company, Company F 51st Infantry

(Long Range Patrol), the 71st Infantry Long Range Patrol Detachment, Company M 75th Infantry (Ranger), the 7th Support Battalion and the 313th Signal Company. Additional units assigned or attached to the Brigade were Fireball Aviation, the 40th Public Affairs Detachment, the 44th Military History Detachment, the 49th Infantry Scout Dog Platoon, the 76th Infantry Combat Tracker Dog Detachment, the 152nd Military Police Platoon, 179th Military Intelligence Detachment, the 298th Signal Platoon, the 503rd Chemical detachment and the 856th Radio Research Detachment.

The 199th Infantry Brigade (Light) unit shoulder patch, shown on the upper left of the cover of this book, is an oblong blue shield representing the Greek Phalanx and the Roman Legion, ancestors of the modern infantry. The spear in flames symbolizes its early use as a weapon. The red ball is the symbol of the Nuclear Age; the yellow flame represents the advent of gunpowder.

The 199th Infantry Brigade (Light) participated in eleven of the seventeen US Army campaigns in the Republic of Vietnam. It also participated in twenty major battles or operations during that time. One of these was the Cambodia Incursion (Sanctuary Campaign) between May 6 and June 27, 1970. The Brigade received five unit awards: The Valorous Unit Award, the Meritorious Unit Commendation, two Republic of Vietnam Cross of Gallantry with Palm, and the Republic of Vietnam Civil Action Unit Citation. Company D 4th Battalion 12th Infantry received the Presidential Unit Citation. From September 1968 to May 1969, the Brigade was commanded by Brigadier General Frederick E. Davison, one of three Black general officers in the US Army at the time and the first to command an active combat brigade. Another commander, Brigadier General William Ross Bond (November 1969 to April 1970)(Panel W12 Line 65), shot by a sniper, was the only commanding officer of the Brigade killed in direct combat in the Republic of Vietnam. He was also the only general officer killed in direct combat during the war. Fire Support Patrol Base Bond (YS625-647) in Phuoc Tuy Province, established on April 20, 1970, was named to honor him. The FSB and Patrol Base accommodated elements of both the 199th Infantry Brigade (Light) and the Australia New Zealand Army Corps (ANZAC).

During its forty-six months in the Republic of Vietnam, the 199th Infantry Brigade (Light) lost 757 soldiers killed in action, 4,679 wounded in action and nine soldiers missing in action. Included in the number of KIA are the 105 soldiers of the 5th Battalion 12th Infantry. PFC Samuel K. Rankins (Panel W7 Line 19) of B Battery 2nd Battalion 40th Artillery, killed on August 28, 1970 in Binh Thuy Province, was the last combat casualty of the Brigade. The following Brigade members were awarded the Medal of Honor: Chaplain (Captain) Charles James (Angelo) Liteky, Headquarters and Headquarters Company 199th Infantry Brigade; Specialist Fourth Class Kenneth Lee Olson (Panel E59 Line 28), Company A, 5th Battalion 12th Infantry; Corporal Michael Fleming Folland (Panel W21 Line 51), Company D 2nd Battalion 3rd Infantry; Sergeant Richard Allen "Butch" Penry, Company C 4th Battalion 12th Infantry. Fifteen Brigade soldiers were awarded the Distinguished Service Cross.

Today, the 199th Infantry Brigade lives on at Fort Benning, Georgia. It is part of the US Army Training and Doctrine Command. Its mission: Develop "committed, adaptive leaders."

In Vietnam, two of the Brigade's battalions, the 4th and the 5th were part of the 12th Infantry Regiment. They were two of the five 12th Infantry Regiment battalions serving in the Vietnam War, the most battalions of any regiment. The 12th Infantry Regiment was constituted in the Regular Army as the 1st Battalion 12th Infantry and activated in 1861. The 12th Infantry Regiment saw action in the US Civil War, participating in eleven campaigns, in the Indian Wars in five campaigns, in the War with Spain, in the Philippine Insurrection in three campaigns, in World War II in five campaigns, in Vietnam in eleven campaigns. It also served in Bosnia, Guantanamo Bay Cuba (JTF-160), Afghanistan, and Iraq.

The 12th Infantry Regiment is highly decorated. With 26 awards including the Presidential Unit Citation (five), the Valorous Unit Award (six), the Meritorious Unit Commendation (seven), the Joint

Meritorious Unit Award, the Belgian Fourragere (1940), the Republic of Vietnam Cross of Gallantry with Palm (four) and is cited in the Order of the Day of the Belgian Army twice (Belgium, Ardennes). The Regiment's actions in the Ardennes earned it the motto "Having Led by Love of Country."

The 12th Infantry Regiment Distinctive Unit Insignia (upper right on the book cover) tells the regimental history from the US Civil War to the Spanish American War. The field of blue symbolizes the infantry. The crosses recall the devastating losses at Gains Mill during the US Civil War. The wigwam with its five poles represents the five campaigns in the Indian Wars in which portions of the regiment participated. The upper third of the shield depicts the Spanish and Philippine wars. Red and yellow were Spain's colors, and red and blue were the colors of the Katipunan, a Philippine revolutionary society founded in Manila in 1892. The embattlements portray the blockhouse at El Caney. (Spanish-American War: Fought July 1, 1898. Five hundred and fourteen Spanish regulars with 100 Spanish and Cubans held off 6,899 of the US 5th Infantry Division consisting of the 12th and 25th Regiments.) The lion with the sword represents the arms of the Philippine islands. The crest commemorates the capture of the Spanish flag at El Caney.

The Combat Infantry Badge or CIB (top center on the book cover) is an award presented to the combat infantryman or Special Forces operator in designated specialties "who satisfactorily performs infantry duties, is assigned to an infantry unit engaged in ground combat and who actively participates in ground combat." The War Department established the Badge on October 27, 1943, retroactive to December 7, 1941. It was designed to enhance morale and the prestige of the infantry. It consists of a three-inch-wide rectangular bar with an infantry-blue field. Superimposed on that field is a War of Independence-era Springfield Arsenal Musket, Model 1795. The composite device is married to an elliptic oak-leaf wreath, symbolizing steadfast character, strength, and loyalty. Of all the awards and decorations an infantry soldier may have, the Combat Infantry Badge is the most cherished and the most envied.

The Fire Support or Fire Support Patrol Base, FSB for short, was an installation, as the name implies, providing artillery support to the infantry. These semi-permanent bases had different configurations depending on location and mission. Early in the Vietnam War, an FSB moved every two or three days. Later in the War, it was not uncommon to see permanent well-fortified locations. Typically, the FSB had a Field Artillery battery of either 105MM (Towed) howitzers or 155MM (Towed) howitzers. These were generally flown into the FSB by the Boeing CH-47 Chinook or the Sikorsky CH-54 Tarhe helicopters. On some occasions, the FSB might be small, highly mobile, and configured around the 4.2-inch (107MM) mortar or the 81MM mortar. Generally, the FSB had a tactical operations center (TOC) and aid station, a communications bunker. Sometimes engineers were assigned to maintain the fortifications and defensive wire. An infantry company defended the FSB while its battalion's other companies conducted operations within range of the batteries. FSBs were named for officers and enlisted, wives and daughters, and historical figures. For example, FSB Deeble (YT949-265) Binh Tuy Province, named in honor of 1st Lieutenant James Frederick Deeble (Panel 11 Line 21) who was killed in action on April 18, 1970 while serving in C Battery 2nd Battalion 40th Artillery 199th Infantry Brigade (Light). And FSB Gladys (YT256-275), origin unknown, located on the Song Dong Nai River and home to elements of the 5th Battalion 12th Infantry and the 2nd Battalion 40th Artillery 199th Infantry Brigade (Light).

The US Army in South Vietnam suffered from the age-old problem: generals preparing for a future war with a strategy and the tactical doctrine of the past. At the time, the US Army was organized and trained to fight a major land war, perhaps nuclear, on the continent of Europe to repel and overcome a Soviet attack. That scenario would re-fight World War II defending the Fulda Gap, dependent upon heavy armor and mechanized infantry with air and theater missile support. South Vietnam was another story. Prepared for conventional warfare and using a strategy of attrition, the US Army was not prepared for counterinsurgency operations, let alone jungle warfare. It was also not equipped to deal with the corrupt leadership of the Republic of Vietnam Armed Forces, forcing it to shoulder the heavy burden of combat operations. It adapted (i.e., Airmobile) and had major and significant battlefield successes. In the end, the US Army left South Vietnam in 1975 a tactical winner but defeated by its philosophy and operational strategy, politics both internal and external, and a Congress and populace tired of war. Fast forward to Iraq and Afghanistan in the 21st century, and the lessons of Vietnam still appear unlearned.

When locations are cited they will have, if available, an alphanumeric grid location within parentheses.

The alphanumeric after a soldier's name refers to the name's location on the Vietnam Memorial.

PART 1
OPENING SALVO

> *A story has no beginning or end: arbitrarily one chooses that moment of experience from which to look back or from which to look ahead.*
>
> Graham Greene

IN FEBRUARY 2020, I met a Vietnam veteran who served two tours in South Vietnam. The first was in 1968 during the Tet Offensive and the second in 1970 during the Cambodia Incursion. In the conversation, we discovered a mutual acquaintance, one with whom we both served in Vietnam but at different times. A few hours after arriving home, the phone rang. At the other end was the acquaintance, a platoon leader in 1968 in the same company as the veteran I met and a captain (my company commander) during his second tour in 1970. It was a good but short conversation. We recalled some of the crazy things that happened during the four and a half months we served together, and he set the record straight on one other. Toward the end of the conversation, he mentioned a book that he published and suggested that I write about my Vietnam experiences.

Several days later, armed with an eighteen-year-old single-malt

Scotch, I retrieved files of notes and musings that I had written over fifty years, along with the few fading photographs I took in Vietnam. My writing over the years was never intended to be a book. It was meant to be cathartic. Some of the contents of those writings are funny, others are solemn, and others are about the Vietnam war in general: the feelings, the politics, the absurdity, and the gallows humor. I also found the Boonie (bush) hat and the last pair of jungle boots I wore in Vietnam, along with the ribbon rack and Combat Infantry Badge that I wore after returning from Vietnam.

Over the years, I studied wars and warfare, especially the Vietnam War. I'm not surprised that combatants, professional historians, amateur historians, and others viewed similar situations differently. Participants in the same action seemed to remember the circumstances differently. There are embellishments, war stories, and things are left out as perhaps too harrowing, embarrassing, or frightening. Then there are the novelists (and the historians) who took creative license and wrote stories containing composite characters and compressed timelines. Screenwriters adapted these books or developed a storyline out of whole cloth, most often to support an antiwar or anti-military agenda.

On the other hand, the combatant had the immediate up close and personal experience of the sights, the smells, the noise, the horrendous wounds, and the death associated with combat. Images and sensations that combat veterans never forget. By various mechanisms, most combat veterans did well and reintegrated into society almost seamlessly. Others just cannot overcome the demons. Alcoholism, drug dependency, failed relationships, broken marriages, and suicide follow, most often in that order. As I read through the accounts by others of actions in which I participated, I wondered if I was there at all. My recollections are different. My memory is not better than theirs; it is just different. As for demons, mine are fewer as the years progress.

PART 2
THE BEGINNING – 1968

The soldier is the Army. No army is better than its soldiers. The Soldier is also a citizen. In fact, the highest obligation and privilege of citizenship is that of bearing arms for one's country.

General George S. Patton Jr.

Holy Crap!

IT STARTED ON a March morning in 1968. An envelope arrived at my Oxnard, California address inviting me to join a select group of individuals at the Ventura County Selective Service Office (Draft Board). I'm drafted. My draft category was 4-A, the sole surviving son. According to induction statistics for 1968, the select group numbered 296,406 that year. One million eight hundred fifty-seven thousand three hundred four draftees (68.6%) out of a total of 2,707,918 served during the Vietnam War.

I'd known that I'd be in the Armed Forces, most likely the Navy at some point. My father and one of his brothers were career Navy men, and my mother's brother served in the Navy in World War II. With my family history, I appeared destined to serve, but as it turned out, not on my terms. With not-so-stellar grades in college, the Navy at the time wasn't taking warm bodies. The other Services didn't appeal to me. I didn't enlist. I worked for a defense contractor as a draftsman and then as an offset platemaker and quality control. The Draft was my future. Years later, with maturity and discipline gained through military service, I obtained two graduate degrees.

On an April 1968 morning, I'm standing in the warm sun with others at the Ventura County Selective Service Office, waiting for the bus to take us to Los Angeles. My dad is there to see me off. My mother and sister decided to stay home. There are friends or relatives of the others there also.

The Vietnam War has raged since the early 1960s. The country had spent eight years, in short segments, hearing about the war on the CBS Evening News with Walter Cronkite. Coverage alternated between war correspondents in Vietnam and the college campus and Draft Board protests. It wasn't at all intense, as I recall. That changed in January and February 1968. The stark images on TV of the fighting during the Tet Offensive brought home the sheer savagery of the war. After Cronkite denounced the war, the tide of public opinion turned, and the protests became more prominent and more frequent. In 1968 there were twenty major protests; 1969 had seventeen major protests; 1970 had eighteen major protests. Some were violent, as in the bombing of the Pentagon and at several recruiting stations. Some were large, with over 100,000 people attending. Most had people burning draft cards and American flags. More than a few had Vietnam veterans returning their medals as a form of protest.

Mostly in silence, we made the ninety-minute bus ride down the Pacific Coast Highway to Los Angeles. The few who knew each other conversed in low tones, mostly about girlfriends, surfing, and other pleasures. Some with a view of the Pacific Ocean looked at the scenery for what may be the last time. We knew we were going to Vietnam, whether as infantry or some other specialty. Some seemed eager to get it over with and get back to civilian life. For the rest, this was not the adventure that we dreamed of while growing up. Those

PART 2 THE BEGINNING – 1968

nightly newscasts of the Vietnam War and the draft protests on the college campuses and in Washington DC now weighed heavily on our minds.

We arrived in Los Angeles at the Armed Forces Entrance and Examination Station (AFEES), full of anticipation and uncertainty. We were herded with others from Southern California, some of whom were enlistees, into a large room with student desks and given a battery of qualification tests. Under the watchful eye of our keepers, we moved to medical stations for physical evaluations and vaccinations. Several guys tried unsuccessfully to beat the Draft by faking medical or psychological conditions or pushing the societal taboos of the time. There was some good-natured horsing around. One incident involved a guy who was afraid of needles. Just talking about needles made him anxious. His buddies knew this and joked about the pain. As a result, he panicked and passed out even before the shot was administered. Everyone, including the military personnel, had a good laugh at his expense. The incident provided a much-needed break from the reality of our circumstances.

We dressed and returned to the big classroom. An officer came in and administered the oath. We were sworn into the Armed Forces of the United States. At this point, it sunk in. We were now, for good or bad, depending on one's perspective, in the service of our county. There was no turning back.

Shortly, a wiry, full-of-himself US Marine Corps captain entered and told us that it was indeed a sad day for his Marine Corps. The Corps, it so happened, had the authority to accept men from the draft pool. He, however, wanted volunteers. The Corps preferred volunteers. To everyone's surprise, one soul immediately stood up and volunteered. The captain was delighted. Then, silence. No one else volunteered. The captain, in a somber tone, told us that with no further volunteers, he'd call a name, and that person was bound for the Marine Corps. No appeal. With no additional volunteers, the captain called three names. With a look of defeat on their faces, the three men slowly got up and moved toward a lance corporal. They were escorted away. With a smirk on his face, the captain followed. At this time, there was a commotion among three draftees in the room. The captain had called their friend's name. The four had promised each other that they would serve together in the Army. Now they were split up, and a decision hung over them like a dark cloud.

The captain returned after a short interval and again asked for volunteers. There being none, he continued with the roll call of future Marines. The captain began with the name of the guy in front of me. Then the name of the guy to my right. Then the name of the guy to my left. Finally, the name of the guy behind me. My world shrunk, and the room grew hotter. I realized that with one more name called, I would be a Marine. In artillery terms, I was bracketed, as in bracketing the target. The calling of names paused. Simultaneously, the three buddies stood up and volunteered for the Corps to be with their friend. The captain met his quota of new "recruits." The rest of us remained silent and relieved. "Oh, happy day!"

Basic Combat Training and Beyond

It was late when we boarded buses for the 340-mile trip north on US 101 to the basic training base at Fort Ord on Monterey Bay, California. We did not know the destination, making the five-hour trip in the darkness seem much longer. We made one stop at Buellton to stretch our legs.

We arrived at the reception center in the early morning hours, and we were hustled off the bus, given a meal, shown our bunks, and sent to bed. What seemed like minutes later, we awoke to shouts. Once dressed, we formed up under the watchful eyes of the drill sergeants and marched, such as it was, to the barbershop for the rite-of-passage haircut and then on to clothing and equipment issue. It was just like the movies, only up close and personal. Thus began the dehumanizing process of breaking us down, removing the civilian in us, and making us fighting machines for the Vietnam War.

We marched from the clothing issue warehouse to a classroom

PART 2 THE BEGINNING – 1968

for orientation and a series of tests. More tests! Each test was immediately graded, after which a Specialist Fourth Class (SP4) called names. Those called were ushered out the door. After the last test, fifteen remained in the room. We looked around, and each of us seemed to register the same thought: "We are the dumbest SOBs in the entire group." Our assumption wasn't valid. A lieutenant informed us that we qualified for Officer Candidate School (OCS), and the school was ours if we wanted it. "Hell yeah!" We were separated from the larger group and assigned to a different basic training company.

While awaiting transfer to our new company, the fifteen ended up at the reception center's holding company. We are "duty soldiers" doing any odd make-work job that the cadre devised. The odd jobs don't matter. The jobs take us away from the misfits and malcontents—a cast of characters out of a Fellini film, with medical, personal, or psychological problems. A few are awaiting pick-up by civilian law enforcement. One guy sits hunched over in a corner, rocking back and forth, rubbing the bridge of his nose raw. Another acted like he owned the place and bullied a fair number of the weaker boys. Years later, as a captain, I would revisit this place while conducting a UCMJ (Uniform Code of Military Justice) Article 32 Investigation. The Article today is distinctly different than the Article in the 1970s. The Fiscal Year 2014 National Defense Authorization Act, Section 1702 changed the Article from an "Investigation" to a "Public Hearing."

That night we hardly slept. With our gear against the wall and mess knife in hand, we anticipated the inevitable attempt at robbery or beating. Thankfully, neither happened. The night was a character-builder and a test of looking out for one's buddy. Late the next day, we shipped to Company C (Charlie) 2nd Battalion 1st Brigade or C-2-1 to start eight weeks of basic infantry training.

And so the "fun" began. C-2-1 was housed in a concrete barracks building on what was known as the "Hill"— Kelly Hill, I think. Each barrack floor was an open bay, with double bunks on each side of the aisle with two footlockers on the aisle in front of bunks. Communal showers and toilet facilities were on one end, and the cadre room and CQ (Charge of Quarters) were at the other end. We were rotated through the various leadership positions during our eight weeks in the company.

Sergeant First Class Carbone and Sergeant Dinkins are standout drill sergeants. Carbone is a short, wiry Filipino, Korea and Vietnam combat veteran, and senior drill sergeant. He has a star on his Combat Infantry Badge. Dinkins is the platoon drill sergeant. Both embody the qualities that we future officers will look for in the non-commissioned officers with whom we'll serve.

Fort Ord, for the basic trainee, is not a garden spot. The weather appeared to change each hour from damp fog to hot sun and back again. The terrain in the training areas was mainly sand, scrub oak and tumbleweed. Some days it felt cold enough to snow. When the wind blew off of Monterey Bay, the sand got into everything. Mostly we trudged through the fog season, the sun season, the rainy season, and at times it seems all of those "seasons" in one day over the eight weeks.

Our training is designed to rid us of our civilian ways and thinking, tearing us down mentally and physically and building into us a military mindset ready for integration into the "Mean Green Fighting Machine." There are physical, academic, and moral standards. There is harassment and hazing. All are designed to instill in us the warrior ethos and bring out latent leadership qualities. So, we make our beds with hospital corners and fold our socks and underwear precisely. We clean our barracks and polish the floors to a brilliant shine each morning before breakfast. Later we may come back after lunch and find the barracks turned upside down. The cleaning starts again. It is a recurring theme. Character building, it's called. Perfect training for OCS. In addition to housekeeping, we learned hand-to-hand combat, the fundamentals of unarmed fighting, designed to instill confidence in our ability to protect ourselves against an armed or unarmed enemy. We received tactical, CBR (Chemical Biological and Radiological) training and familiarization with the M26A1 "Lemon" hand grenade, a replacement for the "Pineapple" grenade of World War II and Korea.

PART 2 THE BEGINNING – 1968

Later, in Vietnam, we had the M61 "Baseball" grenade—a rounded, smoother, lighter version of the M26A1.

In the fourth week, we were issued an M-14 7.62MM rifle. It is our best friend. On occasion, we sleep with it. We memorized the serial number, and are prepared to repeat it if asked by the drill sergeant or officer. If we can't remember it or hesitate in the slightest, we do push-ups. We learned rifle drill, bayonet drill, and close hand-to-hand combat, the care and cleaning of the rifle, and finally, marksmanship.

Our introduction to marksmanship took place in our fourth week at what was called the inland range complex. The complex housed several ranges that provided training in small arms and recoilless rifles and included areas for maneuver training of squad-sized units. We trained at several of these ranges. We learned the characteristics of the M-14 rifle: the weight (9.2 lbs. empty; 10.7 lbs. w/loaded detachable box magazine), the length (44.3 inches), the cartridge (7.62X51MM NATO), the rate of fire (700-750 rounds per minute), the muzzle velocity (2800 feet per second) and sighting (effective range 500 yards, maximum range 3725 yards). We learned to take it apart and put it back together over and over until we could do it in our sleep. When I got to Vietnam, I was issued a much lighter M-16A1 5.56MM rifle. The basic principles of cleaning, maintenance, and marksmanship are the same. I couldn't imagine humping the M-14 through the jungle.

After our introduction to the rifle, we moved to the live-fire phase of rifle training, conducted on the beach range complex more than a mile from the barracks. A series of ten rifle ranges west of California Route 1 facing Monterey Bay with the city of Monterey on the left (south) and a Spanish-style Serviceman's club named for Brigadier General Joseph "Vinegar Joe" Stillwell, on the far right (north).

To get to the ranges, we marched, double-timed, or flat-out ran on a trail made of sand and in one area composed of pierced-steel planking from an old east-west World War II runway. The drill sergeants kept us in the sand most of the way. After exiting the tunnel under Highway 1, we see Monterey Bay and turn left to Range #1. In a week and a half, we fire our rifle on the ten ranges in the beach complex.

One day the monotony of repetitive firing was interrupted when a deer appeared atop a dune at 300 meters from the firing line. It looked majestic and appeared to challenge us defiantly. The call "Cease Fire!" rang out, and range personnel decided what to do. One NCO instructor took a rifle and climbed the range tower and, with great flair, proceeded to show us his prowess as a "real" marksman. He failed. He took multiple shots at the unmoving deer, missing low every time. Showing its disdain, the deer snorted, shook its head, and moved deliberately out of sight. The NCO suffered a humiliating barrage of comments and laughter from the cadre and smirks from the trainees. He responded that the shot was difficult to even the best marksman at that distance and with a breeze coming off the Bay. He told us that he deliberately missed it. He was only trying to scare the beast into leaving so that training could continue. No one bought his story. We resumed firing.

At the end of a long final day of qualification, the company double-timed back to the barracks from Range #10, the farthest range. It wasn't pretty. Before the company reached the abandoned runway, several soldiers dropped out. The drill sergeants pushed harder and, as punishment, made us low crawl through the sand. More soldiers dropped out, eliciting more yelling from the drill sergeants. One squad leader was half running, half crawling to the back of the formation to pick up stragglers. Stopping at one, he threateningly grabbed a soldier's shirt collar and, in low tones, told him that if he didn't move now, he'd never move again. The soldier got the point, and with some effort and the help of the squad leader, he marshaled his last reserves and moved forward. The squad leader brought up the rear of the formation, collecting stragglers and encouraging them to move forward. By this time, everyone knew that they didn't want to be the last man. They moved quickly when the squad leader got near them. The drill sergeants eventually had everyone standing and slowly walking to North-South Road and gave the company a ten-minute break. There were no further incidents and no further punishments. In

PART 2 THE BEGINNING – 1968

silence, except for the cadence call, the company marched back to the barracks as if nothing happened. At the barracks, I was told by our drill sergeant that I did a good job motivating the stragglers but that I shouldn't try the same approach in Vietnam.

Two hundred and twenty-four soldiers graduated from C-2-1 in June 1968. Of those, twelve died in South Vietnam. After graduation, most remained at Fort Ord for AIT (Advanced Individual Training). The fifteen future officers received orders for branch officer candidate school. While some branch assignments changed, I remained infantry. After Vietnam, I returned to Fort Ord and the Training Command (Provisional) as a training officer. I experienced Basic combat Training from the trainer's perspective.

Before heading to Fort Benning, Georgia for OCS, my initial assignment was Fort Bragg, North Carolina, and Detachment D 15th Military Intelligence Battalion (Aerial Reconnaissance Support)(Field Army). This assignment was based on my military occupational specialty (MOS) 86G Photographic Laboratory Specialist. Because I didn't have a security clearance, I was a duty soldier, meaning that I was on kitchen police (KP) duty or guard duty most of the time, and when not doing that, I swept floors and stayed out of other people's way. My best memory of this assignment was walking guard duty around the bakery a 0400 (4:00 AM). Now, sometimes when I smell the aroma of fresh cinnamon rolls and brewing coffee, I'm reminded of that time.

During my time at Fort Bragg, I was being observed as part of the OCS screening process. My section chief, a Warrant Officer, and the detachment commander, a 1st lieutenant, suggested that I relinquish my OCS start date and commissioning, remain with the battalion, obtain training as a photo interpreter, and delay my assignment to Vietnam. The main enticement is that I'm not in the field as a photo interpreter in Vietnam, and I have three hot meals and a bed with sheets ("three hots and a cot" in GI lingo). They tested my commitment to OCS. While the offer is tempting, I don't accept.

19 MILES

Georgia on My Mind

> *Far across the Chattahoochee to the Upatoi,*
> *Proudly stands our alma mater, Benning school for boys.*
> *Onward ever backward never faithfully we stride,*
> *To the ports of embarkation, Follow Me with pride.*
>
> OCS Alma Mater 1969

Fort Benning is located outside of Columbus, Georgia. It is situated between the Chattahoochee River and Upatoi Creek. I was there as both an officer candidate and as a commissioned officer between August 1968 and November 1969.

In 1968, OCS was twenty-three weeks of physical and mental training focusing on combat leadership essentials, weapons and weapons systems, and infantry tactics, with other military subjects thrown in for good measure. In 1942, OCS was thirteen weeks long, leading to the moniker of the OCS commissioned officer as a "Ninety-Day Wonder." As in 1942 and probably in today's OCS, discipline was front and center. Daily infractions of the rules and the "gigs" (black marks) that accrued were common. Punishment might be immediate, like doing push-ups or sitting in the "green chair" (squatting, back against the wall, knees at a 90° angle and holding the position until thoroughly chastised) or walking "tours" on the basketball court while your fellow candidates had free time. Clothing and equipment had their place and space. Shoes in a specific position, hangers so many inches apart, beds made a certain way. TAC officers measured every distance and length. There was no compromise. Our appearance was also measured: from the shine on the helmet liner, the positioning of the decals on the helmet liner and positioning of the helmet liner on our head, to the position of the collar brass, and the angle of our feet when at attention or parade rest. Details. Everything was in the details. "Pay attention to detail," we constantly heard. "Overlooking the

PART 2 THE BEGINNING – 1968

smallest detail will get you and your unit killed" was another warning. Truer words were never spoken.

It was hot and muggy in late August 1968 when I arrived for OCS in-processing at 66th Company 6th Battalion The Candidate Brigade (Provisional). I wore my issued wool uniform and because of this, sweated profusely. I didn't make a good first impression on the Tactical Officer (TAC) who greeted me at the barracks door. Thus began the numerous push-ups and punishment tours that passed as character building throughout my time in OCS. I later learned after OCS that Benning, despite the summer weather, is a pleasant place for assignment or even house arrest.

Others arriving with me experienced similar hazing. Some were fresh from AIT; others, like me, had no AIT but short assignments after basic training. Others had prior military experience as non-commissioned officers, and several of those with Vietnam experience. None of this mattered; we were all in the same boat, starting from scratch, and the following twenty-three weeks felt like basic training on steroids. The officer candidates today attend for twelve weeks. They don't know what fun they're missing.

Physical fitness and framing the proper mental attitude were a significant part of preparing us to be officers. Other courses and classes made up the curriculum. There was the Leadership Reaction Course, designed to assess teamwork, decision-making, and leadership. There were firepower demonstrations. And then there are classes: the proper techniques for clearing mines and booby traps (today's improvised explosive devices); supply and logistics; airmobile landings, tactics, and takeoffs; calling for and adjusting artillery and mortar fire; communications; and map reading and land navigation. In one class we were required to leave a protective trench and low-crawl under barbed wire while live machine gun rounds flew overhead. This class was conducted under both day and night conditions. Finally, there were tactical exercises such as search and destroy operations and attacking a fortified Vietnamese village.

Some in my OCS company did not finish. Injury, mental stress,

19 MILES

and academic failure were common. Other reasons were general incompetence and arrogance, as both lead to unnecessary deaths in combat. All of us knew that failure was not an option; orders for Vietnam would follow.

The two most widely failed academic subjects were land navigation and tactics. During my time, candidates failing these subjects were removed from OCS altogether, recycled back to the instruction cycle where remedial training was needed, or recycled back to zero-week. Unfortunately, I had a problem with land navigation (I could read a map, I just couldn't navigate well) and also needed an attitude adjustment, so I was recycled back to zero-week from week fourteen. I ended up in the 94th Company 9th Battalion (Class 501-69). The company area faced the three large jump towers with an encircling track. Occasionally, we ran on that track. The Battalion was jokingly and derisively called the "Champagne Battalion," meaning it was "soft." This wasn't true. The training and harassment were similar to my experience in 61st Company.

There was more pressure on me now, having completed about 60% of the program to date. I knew the system, I knew what the TAC could and could not do, and I passed that information to the platoon. My problem with authority and lack of tact (diplomacy; avoids giving offense) followed me and became more evident, but somehow I managed to rise from a "1" in "Tact" (the lowest score) to a "2" by graduation. My outspokenness followed me my entire career and led to some pretty interesting situations.

The best part of our training was outdoors at the ranges and away from Building 4 (also known as "Bunker 4" or "Bedroom 4"), where the classroom training was held. We learned almost every nook and cranny of the outer Post during OCS. We marched, double-timed and flat-out ran the roads and trails. The best part? Rain or shine, Howard showed up with his ice cream truck and sold us our favorites. Mine was a pint of black cherry ice cream.

The day finally arrived, swearing-in as an officer (2nd Lieutenant, Military Occupational Specialty 1542, Small Unit Leader) of Infantry

PART 2 THE BEGINNING – 1968

in the US Army. During the weeks before graduation, we received assignment orders. Some were slated to go to Jungle School in Panama; others would get follow-on training at Airborne or Ranger school, usually both; others would go to non-infantry branch-related training; still, others would be assigned to state-side or overseas units in Germany or Korea. However, many times these orders would change, not once but several times. In my case, I first received orders to the 3rd Infantry (Old Guard). These orders were rescinded and changed to airborne, Ranger, Special Forces. My final orders upon graduation assigned me to the 199th Infantry Brigade (Light), Republic of Vietnam with a layover at Fort Benning.

For the final parade of OCS, I was part of the battalion staff. As the Adjutant, I was required to align the guides and march most expeditiously to the front of the battalion formation. Those with first-hand experience know the difficulty of fast-walking from the edge of the parade field to a point at the center of the formation and doing it with dignity. For those observing, it can be a hilarious spectacle. The TAC officers made sure that I got it right. They made me practice the walk and my command voice at every opportunity. Everywhere we marched, I called cadence. When it suited them, the TACs would have me "call the battalion to attention," usually repeatedly until I was hoarse. On many occasions, both the walk and command voice were required to enter the chow hall. I would often reach for my tray only to hear, "Go back and do it again!" Unfortunately, I misstepped. But recovered and, with dignity intact, completed my assignment.

After leave in California, I reported to The Candidate Brigade (Provisional) for assignment. Fortunately for me, during in-processing, I dodged a bullet. It seemed I was destined to be a TAC officer. Number one on the list, they told me. However, a classmate of mine, now assigned to the S-1 (Administration/Personnel), placed my file at the bottom of the pile. As the last to be interviewed, I got the only position left to fill, the transportation officer slot in Brigade S-4 (Supply/Logistics).

The assignment was fortuitous. I was interviewed by the S-4

(Supply and Logistics), a major, a person who would interview me for an advisor's job in South Vietnam in September of 1970. The major handed me over to a crusty (is there any other kind) CW4 (chief warrant officer), who introduced me around the office. The last stop was the area where I would work. I faced three grey metal desks positioned in front of a map of Fort Benning. Sitting behind the desk on the left is a 1st lieutenant who was the logistics/supply officer. The middle desk was reserved for the transportation officer, and it was mine. Behind the desk on the right sat a sergeant E-5. He wore a Combat Infantry Badge (CIB) and the patch of the 1st Cavalry Division.

The chief pointed to the sergeant and said, "This is Sergeant Jay; you'll be working for him for the next few months." Seeing the expression on my face, the chief repeated what he just said and added that my job was to learn how to be an officer. Learning transportation is just the vehicle (pun intended). The chief, with a laugh, turned away; the sergeant grabbed his hat and motioned me to follow him. My education began when I stepped out of the building.

Sergeant Jay (not his real name) served with the 1st Cavalry in the Ia Drang Valley in 1965, where he was wounded. Sergeant Jay was a patient teacher who overlooked the wet-behind-ears naivete of the 2nd lieutenant in front of him. During our time together, he corrected misconceptions and glorifications regarding combat; stressed knowing the job of each soldier, his strengths, limitations, and capabilities; and, as the platoon leader, knowing the job of each infantryman better than the soldier himself did. These and a few other things like gaining trust, being firm and fair. Also, not being an asshole, which would get me killed, and not by the enemy. In other words, being a competent and capable leader who would get the platoon through the uncertainties of war and bring the platoon members home alive and in one piece at the end of their tour.

In addition to my transportation-related duties, I served on inspection teams. These teams inspected the administration and supply operations of the OCS companies and were precursors to inspector-general inspections. My area of "expertise" was the company arms

PART 2 THE BEGINNING – 1968

room. It was a powerful position for a 2nd lieutenant. Years later, I was a civilian division chief in the Mobilization and Operations Directorate of the US Army Personnel Command at the Hoffman Building in Alexandria, Virginia. I stepped into an elevator and spotted a familiar face. It was an officer, now colonel, who commanded an OCS company subject to a brigade-level inspection on which I was a team member. He recognized me as the 2nd lieutenant who failed his arms room. The look on his face indicated that he might still harbored ill will.

PART 3
SOUTH VIETNAM – 1970

The war in the Republic of Vietnam (RVN) was a war for the control of the population...

Command History 1970 Vol III,
MACV HQDA (DAMH-HSR-D),
Center for Military History, Washington DC

Cam Ranh Bay

IN EARLY JANUARY 1970, I'm on a flight from March Air Force Base in Southern California to South Vietnam. It's a long flight broken up by stops in Seattle-Tacoma, Washington; Anchorage, Alaska; and Yakota, Japan before landing at Cam Ranh Bay, South Vietnam. I don't remember much about the flight.

Cam Ranh Bay was hot and humid, not unlike Fort Benning in August and September. For the next two weeks, along with the other newbies, I "acclimatized." Along the way, I was fed information about conditions within the country: weather conditions, supply conditions, combat conditions, medical conditions, morale conditions,

PART 3 SOUTH VIETNAM – 1970

etc. As I recall, there wasn't much emphasis regarding the people and the culture except for the chewing of the betel nut, which stains the mouth a bright red. History was non-existent. I was told how the Viet Cong operated and, later with experience, disregarded many of those lessons. I was familiarized with the M-16 and fire a few rounds downrange. I learned about the flora and fauna of Vietnam especially what was called the deadliest: the Anopheles Mosquito, the spreader of malaria. (US Army malaria-related sick day estimates between 1964 and 1973 were 391,965.) I started the anti-malarial regime of the big orange pill on Monday and the little white pill daily. After two weeks, I travelled to Long Binh and made a brief stop at the 90th Replacement Battalion.

Camp Frenzell-Jones

I'm assigned to the 199th Infantry Brigade (Light), the parent of D (Dakota) Company 5th Battalion 12th Infantry. The Brigade Main Base (BMB) was Camp Frenzell-Jones (YT056-116) at Long Binh. The base was named for two of the brigade's earliest combat casualties from Alpha Company 4th Battalion 12th Infantry: Specialist Fourth Class Herb Frenzell and Sergeant Billy C. Jones, KIA January 21, 1967. The camp sat on 513 acres and had both fixed and rotary-wing aircraft staging areas and runways. I spent about a week at the Redcatcher Training Center for orientation, in-processing and familiarization with the brigade's area of operation (AO), and its standard operating procedures (SOP). There was more discussion regarding Vietnam flora and fauna. Added this time were the Reticulated Python, the longest snake in the world, and the Malayan Krait, a most dangerous snake. This snake, erroneously, was called the "two-step" snake because a soldier allegedly died after two steps when bitten. Another interesting denizen of the jungle was the Tokay Gecko whose male mating call sounded like "tuck-too." At the training center, I again heard a motivational phrase that I often heard at Fort Ord and Fort Benning, "There are two kinds of soldiers in Vietnam: The quick and the dead."

On the last day of orientation, I grabbed my gear and reported to the Battalion S-1 (Administration), then to the Headquarters and Headquarters Company (HHC) for additional equipment and further instructions and sent off to Dakota Company my home for the next eight months. At the company, I was told: "The helicopter leaves in twenty minutes, drop all but your combat gear and draw ammunition [twenty magazines with twenty rounds each of 5.56MM], smoke grenades, extra canteens, bug juice, water purification tablets, and rations for three days." There was no "company orientation time" before actual field duty. Here I was heading into possible combat with a company and platoon, and in an area I knew nothing about and hadn't had time to assess. "Well, Lieutenant," I thought to myself, "this is a fine mess you've gotten yourself into." My apologies to Laurel and Hardy.

As it turned out, there was no combat. The company commander, a well-respected captain, turned over command to a 1st lieutenant, the former 1st Platoon leader. I was the latter's replacement. The captain departed. Things were a little intense; the lieutenant and I didn't hit it off from the get-go. He couldn't let go of the 1st Platoon, making it difficult to connect with the platoon and establish credibility and trust. One or two guys were loyal to their former platoon leader, and the rest took a wait-and-see attitude regarding the new guy. I'm sure that they hoped that I wouldn't screw things up. Eventually, the 1st Platoon sergeant convinced the acting CO to back off and let the new guy have a shot. The remaining days before we headed back to FSB Gladys were just a walk in the jungle.

At this time, I met SSG Le Van Rang, Rang for short, who was a Kit Carson (Tiger) Scout attached to the platoon. Rang was a Chieu Hoi or defector from the Viet Cong (VC). He was an intriguing character who, over the next several months, appeared and disappeared on his schedule. "Expect me when you see me" might be his catchphrase. Rang did not accompany Dakota to Cambodia. I was sure that there were no scouts with Dakota in Cambodia.

That first night in the field was one of apprehension. Especially

PART 3 SOUTH VIETNAM – 1970

Kit Carson (Tiger) Scout SSG Le Van Rang, Long Khanh Province, South Vietnam 1970, Author's Collection

about living up to my expectations of myself. We went to 50% alert and set rotating shifts at the radio. Unable to sleep, I stayed up through the first two shifts with the soldier monitoring the radio. We talked about the platoon and the company. I needed to get a perspective about my new situation. We shared as much personal information as each seemed comfortable divulging. In the background, as if mocking me, came the sound of a tokay gecko calling "tuck-too, tuck-too." "Fuck you, Fuck you." Despite the humor in it, I think that it was predicting my future in Vietnam.

FSB Gladys

After an uneventful hike in the jungle, Dakota and the 1st Platoon walked into FSB Gladys (YT256-275). Gladys was a beehive of activity in Long Khan province on the Song Dong Nai river; it sat across the river from War Zone D. This was my "home" for the next several months. Much different from Camp Frenzell-Jones in Long Binh.

FSB Gladys was barren, dusty, and dirty. A CH-47 Chinook helicopter with a sling load pallet of 105MM Howitzer ammunition hovered, its double rotors kicking up thick clouds of dust and dirt that got into everything. The platoon headed for its assigned position on the

Bunker #9, FSB Gladys, South Vietnam, 1970, Author's Collection

perimeter and began showering, shaving, and changing into clean uniforms; re-confirming fields of fire; cleaning weapons; sorting through mail and packages; other odds and ends.

Clean clothes and shined boots didn't last long. The humidity and rotor wash gave the freshly laundered clothes and shined boots a well-used just out of the jungle look. The 1st Platoon settled into life on FSB Gladys. The daily routine involved improving fighting positions, burning shit, pulling guard duty, moving things from one place to another and back. In many ways it proved the dictum that combat is long periods of boredom punctuated by short bursts of mayhem. Each evening at dusk the entire base conducted a "Mad Minute," firing flares, crew-served weapons, and small arms into the jungle surrounding the base. We were announcing our presence and daring the enemy.

Given the circumstances and the pace, it was not uncommon for a few soldiers to take one of the small boats out for fishing, water skiing or weapon "test firing." Fishing was no rod, no reel, no net; just a hand grenade in the water, a muffled explosion and fish floating to the surface. Water skis were fashioned from the wood lids of ammunition boxes. It was hilarious watching soldiers try to navigate the river on these. Some were very successful; others not so much, with hilarious outcomes—worthy of *America's Funniest Home Videos*, if it had existed at the time. There was one exception. A 1st lieutenant forward observer from the 2nd Battalion 40th Artillery was a legendary waterskier. Unfortunately, he was killed in action on April 18, 1970.

On my second day at Gladys, several soldiers of the 1st Platoon suggested that I accompany them on a fishing excursion. With nothing pressing, I joined them. I was surprised that they brought an M-60 machine gun. The boat eased into the current and moved to an eddy 100 meters upriver. A grenade dropped over the side and seconds later the muffled explosion was followed by a handful of fish floating to the surface. These were scooped up. The boat moved slightly farther upstream. Another grenade, another scoop of fish. Fishing finished, we moved farther upstream and out of sight of FSB Gladys.

19 MILES

Picking up a water skier on the Song Dong Ni River, FSB Gladys, South Vietnam, 1970, Author's Collection

Twenty-five meters from shore the M-60 burst to life and shredded the riverbank. The radio barked a query; I replied that there was no contact, just a test firing of the M-60. None of us thought anything more of the situation.

Returning to FSB Gladys with the catch-of-the-day, we were met by the battalion command sergeant major. He greeted the boat with a string of expletives detailing how the automatic weapons fire alarmed everyone, especially the Arty guys, and that everyone in the boat was a bunch of jerks (stronger language actually). Then he saw me. He stopped the ass chewing, turned, and walked away shaking his head. Shortly, I was getting hell from the CO who just caught hell from the battalion commander. Later, there were fish on a spit.

Wildlife

Patrolling was monotonous and dangerous. We never knew what was along a trail, around a corner, or in a clump of bamboo. In addition to the heat and humidity and an occasional Viet Cong (VC), mosquitos were another hazard. They seemed so big we joked that one could carry a man off of the field. In Cambodia, we encountered the bigger sister. There were also ants, the vicious red kind usually found in rubber plantations and eye-level nests along jungle trails. Accidentally brushing against one of these nests or cutting one with a machete instantly engulfed the unsuspecting soldier in a horde of biting, stinging ant warriors. Doing "The Dance," the soldier immediately began pulling off equipment and clothes. For those of us who weren't fighting the ants, the sight was hilarious.

In Cambodia, for example, we set up for the night in a relatively flat area surrounded by bamboo. Most of us slept on the ground. We were awakened by a stinging pain caused by a column of ants slicing through our camp. Immediately jumping up, we began The Dance while attempting to find an ant-free location and to keep from yelling and alerting the PAVN to our exact location. As if they didn't already know. Our role model for silence was the tracker dog accompanying our unit. The dog seemed to get the worst of the bites, yet it remained silent. At first light, we could see the path of destruction left by the ants. Ponchos, poncho liners, web equipment and clothes showed evidence of the ant attack.

Bees were another scourge in the jungle. But these attacks were not localized to the immediate vicinity of the nest. No, as the bees attacked, the soldier usually retreated along the column, with bees following, indiscriminately attacking everyone in their path. Soldiers were flailing and swinging their towels to ward off the intruders. After gathering ourselves we would cautiously proceed, ever vigilant for the next nest.

Chickens and wild pigs added to the excitement of a patrol. A chicken might show up and run through an ambush position or startle the point man. The pig usually burst through a perimeter or sets off a trip flare. Both of these activities enhanced the pucker factor.

Snakes were another issue. Several dominated the area: The common cobra, the king cobra, the green tree pit viper, the Malaysian krait, the Malayan pit viper, Russell's viper, and the reticulated python. The last is the only non-poisonous snake. I never saw any poisonous snakes because they were arboreal, nocturnal, or generally avoided humans. There were also scorpions and centipedes.

I did see a python, but not in Vietnam. It was in Cambodia, when a very long and very thick python slithered through the night defensive position. It was hilarious, the creature stopping under the hammock of a soldier with a deathly fear of snakes. The soldier, a city boy through and through, didn't know that the snake was there until his buddies pointed it out. I'd never seen a person flail so much to get out of a hammock without disturbing the snake. Eventually, the snake moved on. It took a while for the soldier to regain his composure.

Let's not forget leeches. There was no escaping from these little buggers. They were primarily found in fresh water but sometimes on dry land. So we had to be careful where we walked and how we dressed; however, no amount of covered flesh or bug juice seemed to matter, as the little creatures were adept at finding their next meal— a meal of fresh blood, blood type unimportant. A leech, left to suck away, could grow quite large as they can take in up to five times their body weight in blood. The things were so icky we burned them off rather than waiting for them to stop eating.

Another Day in a Grunt's Life

FSB Gladys was Dakota's home away from home from January to the end of April. From it, we conducted search operations looking for

PART 3 SOUTH VIETNAM – 1970

a Viet Cong regimental headquarters. It was never found, but there was evidence of enemy activity in the area. On February 9, during operations 21 miles northeast of Xuan Loc, elements of Dakota found and destroyed 25 pounds of rice. In the same area on February 22, elements of Dakota found a leather map case containing medical supplies. Later, in March, Dakota found 30 pounds of rice approximately 18 miles north of Xuan Loc. Operating from different firebases, elements of the 3rd Battalion 7th Infantry, the 4th Battalion 12th Infantry, the 2nd Battalion 3rd Infantry, Delta Troop 17th Cavalry and battalion Recon elements all discovered small cache sites or engaged in short firefights. In one such action on April 1, the brigade commander, Brigadier General William R. Bond, was killed in action during an engagement with an unknown number of enemy forces approximately 26 miles from Xuan Loc.

On February 23, Dakota's 1st Platoon worked along a defoliated and Rhome-plowed area maybe 200 meters wide and 1000 meters long, approximately 20 miles north of Xuan Loc. There was a triple canopy jungle surrounding it. It was a slow slog traversing the area, given that the site was beginning to regrow in a gnarled and tangled fashion. The temperature and humidity remained high, making movement difficult and slow. Inside the jungle's edge, we spotted a trail and cautiously followed it to a complex of six bunkers. The complex appeared to be approximately six months old, with no signs of recent use. We cautiously approached, checking for booby traps, and began to clear each bunker with a hand grenade followed by a spray of bullets. Bunker-clearing completed, we assessed the situation. The complex looked like a way station rather than a defensive position for a base camp. I reported the find. Shortly after, the CO told me to move the platoon to a safe area, as an airstrike would soon destroy the complex and deny the enemy its use.

The platoon retreated safely back to where we first crossed the tangled area, taking cover behind some large, downed trees. Within the hour, a Martin B-57 Canberra bomber approached left to right and dropped two 500-pound bombs. The explosions shook the ground, and large pieces of hot shrapnel traversed the open area and embedded in the tree I was using for cover and in the tree directly behind me. It was a close call, but no one was injured. The platoon recrossed the open space and conducted a bomb damage assessment (BDA). There was slight damage to one side of the complex. So much for destroying the complex.

LT Tomko (with RTOs Williams (left) and Lowe (bottom), Long Khanh Province, South Vietnam 1970, Author's Collection

Anticipating enemy movement in the area, I set up an ambush parallel to a trail leading into the complex. Just prior to sundown, three

PART 3 SOUTH VIETNAM – 1970

figures in military uniforms approached and set up camp just inside the complex. Surprisingly, it didn't register with them that there might be a US unit in the immediate area. I adjusted the ambush to catch them together, and we waited. The ambush started with the explosion of an M-79 round near the unsuspecting soldiers. The 1st Platoon lit up the area with about a minute of rifle and M-60 fire. There was no return fire. I called "ceasefire," and we cautiously approached the kill zone and found one body and a blood trail. It appeared that two of the three escaped. We followed the blood trail until it was too dark. The platoon set up an NDP, and I plotted harassment fires along the supposed exfiltration route. During the night, occasional flares cast an eerie light through the jungle canopy. Artillery fire kept the runner on his toes. It had the same effect on some platoon members, including me.

At first light, the search continued. About seventy-five meters from the ambush site, we found the wounded soldier by a tree next to a stream. He was not in good shape and appeared to have lost a lot of blood from a leg wound. I was surprised that he survived the night. Doc did the best he could, treating the wound and the soldier's pain. I radioed the news to the CO, who by this time was in the bunker complex. Shortly, the command element joined the 1st Platoon and immediately posed for pictures with the prisoner. A helicopter arrived, and the wounded soldier was lifted out via jungle penetrator as a South Vietnamese intelligence officer looked on. I suspect that the prisoner died, since the platoon was credited with two kills. We didn't find the other escapee.

"Sir, This Isn't a Mech Company."

We returned to FSB Gladys. The CO was reassigned. His replacement was a second tour infantry captain. The difference in styles was immediately apparent and welcome. Unlike his predecessor, the new guy seemed to have his act together. He was outgoing and interested in the men in his company. I sensed that he saw his primary mission as ensuring each of us got home alive and in one piece. Over time I would know that he was mission-focused and disinclined to take unnecessary risks. The latter got him in trouble in several months while operating in Cambodia.

His first mission with Dakota was to air assault into a location and conduct reconnaissance operations in the general vicinity for approximately a week. After artillery and gunship prep, Dakota Company landed in a "cold" landing zone (LZ). With the LZ secured, the CO gathered his three platoon leaders and proceeded to brief us on our objectives. Pointing to a spot on his map approximately 500 meters from our current location, the CO said that it was the company's objective for the day. Given the distance, terrain, and time of day, it was unlikely that Dakota would make a third of that distance. The 3rd Platoon leader, half-serious and half in jest, said, "Sir, this isn't a mech company," referring to the CO's previous tour with the 2nd Battalion (Mechanized) 47th Infantry 9th Infantry Division. The CO laughed, had us move 100 meters away from the LZ and set up a company night defensive position. The next day we moved out as individual platoons and conducted cloverleaf patrols in the area. I don't recall any of the platoons reaching the original 500-meter objective.

It's Heavy, and It Kicks Ass!

On this operation, a soldier of the 1st Platoon carried an M1 Thompson .45-caliber submachinegun and a leather ammo case with three thirty-round stick-type magazines. The Thompson was favored by gangsters, lawmen and Hollywood in the 1920s and 1930s during Prohibition and the Great Depression. This soldier was pleased with himself, having scored a "kick-ass" weapon that sprayed death and destruction with its heavy round. What he didn't factor in: carrying the weapon in triple canopy jungle with wait-a-minute vines and stifling conditions in addition to having eight pounds or more of water along with C-rations, a claymore mine, and a few other odds and ends. With his new best friend, he struggled as the weapon grew heavier with each hour.

No wonder. The Thompson weighed 11.5 pounds unloaded, six pounds heavier than the M16A1; his walking point didn't help. Yet, he swore by the weapon even while swearing at it. There was envy amongst some of his platoon mates. Even the CO thought that it was a cool tool. However, the next patrol changed all of that. By the second day of this patrol, the extra weight took its toll. He'd had enough. After encountering ants and bees and unforgiving bamboo, cursing, he threw the Thompson down. The Thompson did kick ass; his ass and not the enemy's. Having proved my point, I moved both him and his Thompson into the back of the formation. The Thompson, in my view, was better for guard duty, urban warfare, and the mechanized infantry. The jungle, not so much. However, it was favored at times by Special Forces and Navy SEALs. After returning to FSB Gladys, the soldier exchanged the Thompson for a lightweight M16-A1.

Not Tin Soldiers and Nixon

The beginning of the Cambodia Campaign. In April 1970, US President Richard M. Nixon set the wheels in motion for the incursion (Sanctuary Campaign) into the People's Army of Vietnam (PAVN) sanctuaries in Cambodia. Both US and South Vietnamese forces would attack and destroy logistics bases located in the Parrot's Beak and the Fishhook salients of Cambodia bordering South Vietnam. The US Air Force stepped up the bombing of the Ho Chi Minh Trail through Laos and Cambodia. The incursion, anticipating a complete withdrawal of US forces and complete turnover of combat roles to the South Vietnamese Army, was part of the Vietnamization program. The decision to invade was not without controversy. It further inflamed the student protests and demonstrations against the Vietnam war, ongoing since the early 1960s. On May 4, 1970, Kent State happened: the Ohio National Guard shot and killed four students during a protest at the University. "Four dead in Ohio," words from the protest and counterculture song "Ohio" by Crosby, Stills, Nash and Young was released that summer and set the tone for the rest of the Nixon administration and the Vietnam war.

Extraction (Not the Dental Kind)

The incursion was about two weeks old when, on the evening of 1 or 2 May, the 5th Battalion 12th Infantry was ordered to rendezvous for pick-up the following day. We arrived at a large open area, designated as the PZ (pick up zone), with other battalion units and waited along the tree line. Shortly, gunships began circling the PZ, followed by a string of Hueys, more than we'd ever seen in the same sky at the same time except for stateside training. Smoke was popped, and the birds descended on the designated areas and extracted units one at a time. Dakota was last. As Dakota's birds lifted off, two figures were seen still on the ground. A miscalculation left me and an RTO kneeling back-to-back, weapons ready, nervously scanning the tree line. A single Huey with gunship escort approached and flared next to us. We boarded and a short time later landed at Camp Frenzell-Jones and joined up with the rest of Dakota.

Anticipation and Anxiety

Time at Frenzell-Jones was spent amid rumors, anxiety, and anticipation. The rumor most prevalent was that the battalion was part of a large, combined US and Army of the Republic of South Vietnam (ARVN) force going into Cambodia. The purpose was to disrupt and destroy large PAVN logistics bases in the Parrot's Beak and Fishhook regions at the Cambodia South Vietnam border. The battalion was part of the Fishhook operation.

Apprehensive and anxious about this operation, we loaded up with gear we thought we needed. These were bayonets, entrenching tools, and the M72A2 LAW (Light Anti-tank Weapon), a one-shot 66MM unguided anti-tank weapon. We added several more to those we already carried and doubled our basic load of ammunition and hand grenades. Since supposedly there were no tanks, the company commander thought the M72A2 LAWs were unnecessary and wondered why we wanted additional LAWs, let alone any LAWs. My thinking was that there would be bunkers, and LAWs would effectively suppress fire from them. But if there were tanks, we were prepared.

We carried LAWs in the first place because of an Army decision, before my arrival, to reorganize infantry companies in Vietnam. The decision eliminated the weapons platoon, moved the 81MM mortars to battalion, and augmented the rifle platoons with a weapons squad. Each platoon now had two M-60 machine guns and an M67 90MM Recoilless Rifle from the weapons platoon.

Three men crewed the M67: a gunner, assistant gunner, and ammo bearer. The M67 was 53 inches long and empty weighed 37.5 pounds. The high explosive (HE) round weighed sixteen pounds, and the anti-personnel (AP) round weighed 10.76 pounds. The platoon carried two HE (high explosive) and four AP (anti-personnel) rounds. Humping the weapon and ammunition through the jungle took its toll. The weapon's length caused it to hang up in the heavy jungle. The additional weight of the recoilless rifle and its ammunition plus equipment tended to slow movement, especially in the jungle. It was not good for platoon morale. After our second patrol, I exchanged the M67 for six LAWs and returned the gun crew to regular infantry duties.

Coincident with this change comes another: adding a third caliber 7.62MM M-60 machine gun, thus increasing the platoon firepower. The 1st Platoon was now the only platoon with three. The extra machine gun was a welcome addition.

The acquisition of this extra M-60 was a study in scrounging ingenuity and one of the better-scrounging stories I have heard in my military career. Allegedly, two members of the 1st Platoon took a Brigade Jeep into Long Binh. Exchanging their fatigue shirt for one with a II Field force patch and sergeant's stripes, they then appropriated a II Field Force Jeep and drove it to the perimeter where the guard towers were located. Carrying a clipboard and looking officious, one solder climbed up the ladder to the guard post, surprising the soldier on duty. He told the guard that the M-60 was scheduled for maintenance. The soldier objected. The officious-looking "sergeant" pointed down the fence line to a ¾-ton truck and stated that the replacement gun was there (actually, it was the chow truck). The soldier signed the "paperwork" and released the M-60 to the "sergeant." The two Dakota soldiers returned the purloined Jeep, removed their disguise, returned to Frenzell-Jones, then hitched a ride to FSB Gladys with the M-60.

Armed with the tools of the trade, the 1st Platoon prepared for the Cambodia Incursion.

PART 4
CAMBODIA May-June 1970

To protect our men who are in Vietnam and to guarantee the continued success of our withdrawal and Vietnamization programs, I have concluded the time has come for action.

President Richard M. Nixon, Washington, 30 April 1970

On May 7, 1970, President Nixon limits the incursion to 19 miles into Cambodia and sets the end date for US participation on or before June 30, 1970.

MAY 1, 1970 – THE CAMBODIA INCURSION

As American withdrawal from South Vietnam proceeded, increasing concern arose over the enemy's strength in the sanctuaries inside nominally neutral Cambodia. When North Vietnamese and Viet Cong forces advanced on the Cambodian capital of Phnom Penh, Lon Nol, leader of the anti-Communist government in Cambodia, appealed for help. President Richard Nixon relaxed the restrictions on moving against enemy bases inside Cambodia. American and allied South

Vietnamese forces began large-scale offensives in Cambodia.

Officially called the Sanctuary Offensive, eight major US Army and South Vietnamese operations took place in Cambodia between 1 May and ending in July with the objective of cutting enemy lines of communication, seizing the sanctuary areas, and capturing the shadowy COSVN (Central Office for South Vietnam). On May 1, 1970, a combined US and Army of the Republic of Vietnam force initiated Operation TOAN THANG 43 in the Fishhook area of Cambodia adjacent to Tay Ninh Province 65 miles northwest of Saigon.

The initial incursion into Cambodia was codenamed Operation ROCK CRUSHER by US forces; it included the US 11th and the ARVN 1st Armored Cavalry Regiments, the 3rd Brigade of the US 1st Cavalry Division (Airmobile) and the ARVN 3rd Airborne Brigade, plus one armor and one mechanized infantry battalion from the US 25th Infantry Division and the 3rd Brigade of the US 9th Infantry Division. The 3rd Brigade of the 1st Cavalry Division (Airmobile) had operational control. The Allied units entered Cambodia from three directions aimed at attacking the COSVN, the enemy command headquarters for operations in the Republic of Vietnam and the control center for enemy operations against the III Corps Tactical Zone (CTZ).

Phouc Binh (Song Be)

Operation BOLD ARCHER and Task Force Shoemaker were underway when Dakota Company received orders to load a C-130 at Bien Hao for the trip to the Bu Dop special forces camp 17 miles northwest of Song Be and approximately 3 miles from the border with Cambodia. Weather and poor landing conditions interfered with the flight plan. Rather than returning to Bien Hoa, the Dakota CO made a deal of "free drinks at the US Air Force Officers Club" with the flight crew to return to Ton Son Nhut Air Base. We landed at Ton Son Nhut; there were no accommodations. The company stacked arms, posted a guard; the officers proceeded to the O-Club while the enlisted, with strict orders not to go to Saigon, were left to the Airmans Club and

PART 4 CAMBODIA MAY-JUNE 1970

other things. Needless to say, several enlisted made it to Saigon and were picked up by the MPs. They remained in custody the rest of the night and the CO retrieved them the next day. The officers? Let's just say that being at the O-Club was better than being wet and miserable or perhaps dead at the end of a slick runway. What happened at the club and afterward, I don't remember. Looking back, the detour was fortuitous. Had we landed in Bu Dop, I think that we would have been in Cambodia sooner.

The next day, May 5, we landed at Song Be (Phouc Binh), Phouc Long Province, South Vietnam. Expecting to deploy immediately into Cambodia, the company filled in for units on and outside the perimeter of the 2nd Brigade 1st Cavalry Division (Airmobile) base of operations. Elements of the 5th Battalion 12th Infantry entered Cambodia between May 11-13. Dakota's introduction to Cambodia wouldn't happen until May 24. The company stayed in South Vietnam conducting reconnaissance and bomb damage assessments (BDA) around FSBs Snuffy and Buttons. The BDAs were a bitch. The jungle was torn apart, and areas of bamboo that on a good day were difficult to traverse became more difficult because of the twisted and intertwined bamboo and other debris. The bomb craters were deep and water-filled. In one instance, conflicting orders from the 2nd Brigade S-3 (Operations) had Dakota make a difficult steam crossing three times in the same area on the same day. It was the best spot of all of the bad spots to cross. The sequence was that we crossed and secured the other side of the stream, took a short break to change socks and dry out equipment; then we received a change of orders to recross the stream to avoid an incoming B-52 strike. Back at the original crossing position, we received the order to recross and continue to the original coordinates and continue the mission. We worked through this area for a couple of days, finding nothing of significance.

This mission ended. Dakota, minus the 1st Platoon, was airlifted to FSB Buttons at Song Be. 1st Platoon was airlifted to Hill 723 (YU184-068) also called Nui Ba Ra or White Virgin Mountain. At 2,415 feet, it is the third-highest peak in South Vietnam. The platoon's mission was to "protect" the signal element manning the communications antenna array and relay station.

The facility atop Nui Ba Ra consisted of a helipad, numerous antennas and microwave dishes, an operations center, and quarters for the signal types and perimeter bunkers for the grunts. Among the numerous extra duties was the ever-popular shit-burning detail. Now shit-burning was important from a hygiene standpoint but not a pleasant duty. The latrines had the bottoms of fifty-five-gallon drums under each seat. The crap was burned daily by mixing it with diesel fuel and stirring continuously until the feces were rendered to ash. It was best not to be downwind.

1st Platoon Dakota Company assisting with the installation of an antenna pole, Nui Ba Ra, Song Be, South Vietnam 1970, Author's Collection

PART 4 CAMBODIA MAY-JUNE 1970

Another job was assisting with erecting of an antenna pole; it took a significant number of supervisors to get the job done—not unlike some public works projects at home.

Through all of this, there was some time to relax. Most time was spent writing letters, sleeping, and the occasional touch football game on the helipad. The opportunity for the USO show, however, was not available to the grunts.

Touch football, Helipad, Nui Ba Ra, Song Be, South Vietnam 1970, Author's Collection

USO, "Georgie Who?"

One would think that pulling duty above the clouds and away from the jungle was a blessing—far from it. From the first that we set foot on the mountain, our keeper, a signal branch captain, had us doing the abovementioned crap duties. His rationale was that "his men" performed a vital service and needed to concentrate on monitoring and expediting signal traffic. Besides, he insinuated, the kind of work that the 1st Platoon was doing, in addition to security, was perfect for the infantry. I relayed this sentiment to my CO. I think he began to find ways to extricate us from our circumstances.

The next day we got word that in the afternoon, the USO was sending some entertainment to the mountain. Unfortunately, the entertainment was for the signal cadre; our job was to provide security. To add insult to injury, I was told to vacate the command bunker, as it was needed for a dressing room. Another concern relayed to my CO, who commiserated and said that nothing could be done.

Shortly after noon, a Huey carrying the entertainers arrived. Two young and very attractive females and an old guy stepped out of the Huey. With the "eye candy" on each arm, the old guy was escorted to the "dressing room" by the signal captain. There are some demands that the signal captain was only too happy to fulfill. And the way he looked at the "round eyes" indicated he thought that he'd be rewarded in a "special way."

The captain left the bunker, and the old guy and his companions got ready for the show. I was taken aside by several of my platoon and asked who the old guy was. I told them that he was George (Georgie) Jessel, an American actor, singer, and comedic entertainer, among other things. They still didn't understand why an old guy with two young chicks was entertaining, but were more pissed that the platoon was excluded. I sensed some sort of revenge.

PART 4 CAMBODIA MAY-JUNE 1970

Payback

The men of the 1st Platoon were fed up with the treatment by our hosts. Without my knowledge, they hatched a plot to scare the crap out of our "oppressors." Around 0430 hours, the distinct sound of a flare followed by a claymore explosion and outgoing small-arms fire pierced those early hours before dawn, rousing the facility. Panic ensued amongst the signal cadre. Awakened, I ran to the perimeter to find the soldiers at the position laughing and joking as they fired their weapons into the dark. I called a "ceasefire" at the same time that the sky above lit up from flares provided by the supporting artillery in the valley below. Two AH-1 Huey Cobra gunships materialized and orbited the mountain. Apparently, the mountain's operation center called for support before checking out the situation. This might have been SOP, but it seemed like overkill. The signal captain was beside himself. He appeared panicked and thought that his compound was being overrun by an enemy force of unknown numbers. I told him that given no incoming fire, it appeared to be a false alarm. At first light, I sent out a patrol to assess the situation. Shortly after disappearing into the tree line, the patrol stopped, set up security, and had breakfast. An hour later, they returned and reported both to me and the captain "no enemy activity" and presented me with a pair of bloodied Ho Chi Minh sandals. The signal captain turned white. I chuckled; the soldiers smiled. I recognized the sandals as ones found during one of our BDAs. Several hours later, I received orders to be prepared for displacement to a new location. The news was welcomed by the platoon; shortly, we rejoined the company. I waited for the ass-chewing or Field Grade Article 15 (under the Uniform Code of Military Justice, a form of non-judicial punishment), neither of which materialized.

Today, Nui Ba Ra is a tourist attraction. A gondola car takes people to the summit. A Radio station with towers occupies the same area that 1st Platoon occupied in 1970.

Crazy and Just Plain Stupid – May 24, 1970

    Gunships circled like raptors searching for prey. Hueys approached the LZ with caution, preparing to off-load Dakota company. Each Huey had the maximum number of infantrymen with gear, making for cramped quarters and precarious seating on the outboard sides. I was seated on the left outboard side with about six inches of ass clinging to the seat when the pilot banked at about 45 degrees in order to line up for landing. The sudden move and the centrifugal force broke the ass-to-seat suction, and I started to slide out of the bird. The soldier next to me grabbed my pack and held me in place until the maneuver was completed. Without his assistance, one lieu-

Landing Zone, Cambodia 1970, Author's Collection

PART 4 CAMBODIA MAY-JUNE 1970

tenant (me) would have skydived from 300 feet and face-planted into the LZ.

Then, our bird hovered above the grass and discharged its cargo of infantrymen. Unbeknownst to the pilot and the soldiers, the grass was about six feet high and hid a small ravine. It surprised us to find that the skid-high drop was more like jumping from the roof of a one-story house. Luckily no one was injured. The first elements secured the LZ.

As the second lift touched down, one bird made an inelegant landing on a tree stump, damaged the underside and split a fuel cell. The troops and crew evacuated, liberating the radios and other gear.

Huey with damaged fuel cell leaking JP-4 lifting off from LZ, Cambodia 1970, Author's Collection

In the distance, we heard the sound of a Huey approaching the LZ. It landed to pick up the downed crew. The pilot of the damaged Huey didn't leave with his crew but raced to the damaged helicopter, started it, and proceeded to lift off while trailing copious amounts of JP4 aviation fuel. Barely making it over the trees, he flew toward his base. We waited with bated breath and fingers crossed, hoping we wouldn't be conducting a recovery mission. I'm told the pilot landed to an unwelcome ass-chewing, among other things.

June 11-12 2000 Bicycles and Other Treasures

Twenty-five miles north of Song Be, five miles inside Cambodia, and 2 miles from FSB Myron (YU039-436) Dakota finds a PAVN logistics base, one of many discovered by the 5th Battalion 12th Infantry. Surprise of all surprises, there are approximately 2000 unassembled bicycles awaiting use as transportation of men and materiel into South Vietnam. During the war, bicycles were the prime method for bringing supplies down the Ho Chi Minh Trail from North Vietnam and as individual transportation within the country. A few hundred meters from this location, Dakota found another site containing even more treasures: 61 120MM rounds, 676 rifle grenades, 4 K-62 radios, 27,000 rounds of AK-47 ammunition, some anti-tank mines, and sacks of rice. The battalion headquarters sent an engineer squad to clear a PZ for backhauling the ammunition and radios and to destroy in place the remaining finds. It didn't go well.

The engineers and their leader aren't prepared. Their equipment isn't properly maintained, and they don't seem to understand the fine art of felling trees and blowing things up. The infantry stepped in and schooled them on both maintenance and tree-felling.

One member of my platoon, from Louisiana with lumber- cutting experience, stepped in and fixed the chainsaw and began to effortlessly fell trees. In the meantime, the leader of the engineers and another engineer made several unsuccessful attempts to fell a large tree with explosives. They couldn't get the correct amount of C-4 explosive and its placement correct. A lot of noise and tree splinters flying everywhere, but the tree defiantly remained in place.

The height of engineer incompetence came regarding the decision to blow the 120MM rounds, the anti-tank mines and hand grenades in the middle of the PZ. There are several versions of this story, and they all end the same way. Fortunately, no one was killed or wounded.

Per instructions from the engineers, we stacked the anti-tank mines with the grenades on top of the 120MM rounds in the middle of the PZ. The leader set the C-4 charge, lit the fuse, and ran to a position of "safety" behind a felled tree perhaps forty meters from the blast area, falling on top of me. We waited for what seemed like forever. After ten minutes, there was no explosion. The engineer kept checking his watch. Still nothing. He said to no one in particular that someone had to go down and check the charge. I reminded him that he was the one who set the charge, so he would be the one to check the charge. Reluctantly he stood up, and as he stepped over the protective cover, simultaneously, a loud explosion sounded followed by the shouting of "incoming" as hand grenades rained down and exploded in the trees. Fortunately, as the smoke cleared, there were no calls of "medic," although there was a lot of cursing. Without much discussion, it was decided that Dakota would finish what the engineers couldn't do, and the engineers, less their equipment, were escorted off the LZ. With them was a Dakota lieutenant, new to the company, whom I don't remember meeting. He was a replacement for the 2nd Platoon leader. He must have screwed up big time.

We hauled the remaining 120MM rounds, mines, and grenades back to the caves and stacked them, along with the engineer's tool kit. The 120MM fuse wells primed, we packed rice bags into the voids and in the cave entrance. We lit the fuse. Shortly, the earth shook, and there was a satisfying muffled sound. We watched as the hillside collapsed.

Combat Is Horrible, Awful and a Nightmare, June 16-22

> *If we survive danger it steels our courage more than anything else.*
>
> Reinhold Niebuhr

Tuesday, June 16

Our introduction to ground combat in Cambodia began on the morning of June 16 as we moved deeper into the PAVN logistics zone. The order to "saddle up" echoed through the company and, as we'd done a hundred or more times before, we draped the ever-present OD towel over neck and shoulders, adjusted web gear, secured ammunition, and lifted rucksacks. We checked each other and assisted where necessary. We moved out slowly and deliberately, scanning the jungle to the front and sides of the formation looking for signs of recent enemy activity and booby traps, hoping for the big score of enemy materiel and praying for no contact.

Operating with Dakota Company was a tracker team attached from the 76th Infantry Combat Tracker Dog Detachment consisting of a team leader, a tracker dog, and dog handler. The platoons moved in parallel. The 1st Platoon and the tracker team were in the center and in the open, following a well-used trail and acting as the base element. The 3rd Platoon and command element were my right flank, concealed by tall grass. The 2nd Platoon was on my left flank just outside of a tree line paralleling a small stream.

The going was slow, easy, and uneventful until the dog alerted near a bridge over a small stream to the front of the route of march. The tracker team leader motioned to me and we scanned the area. There was nothing out of the ordinary, yet the dog was anxious. I radioed the CO and moved an M-60 to the front preparing to provide fire support for the 2nd Platoon as it moved to cross the bridge. The

PART 4 CAMBODIA MAY-JUNE 1970

3rd Platoon, still concealed, was in no position to provide supporting fires. I took my position with the fire support element when the report of several small explosions and rapid gun fire erupted to my front. The exchange was short and violent. The firing stopped and I moved to the last known position of the tracker team. The team leader, Frederick Richard Levins of Naples, Florida was KIA (killed in action). The dog and handler were severely wounded. One of my men and one soldier from the 2nd Platoon were also wounded.

I relayed that information to the CO and moved back to my position during the ambush. There, very close to that position, was a dud rifle grenade. It was centered between a point once occupied by me and my RTO. If it had exploded on contact, there would have been two more casualties. Shaken, neither me nor my RTO felt comfortable for the rest of the day. In fact, it took a while to put it behind me.

A Huey hovered and dumped ammunition and water and then dropped a jungle penetrator to evacuate the dead and wounded. Replenished, Dakota crossed the stream at another location and climbed a twenty-foot incline to reach high ground to regroup and establish a NDP. The climb was intense. Knowing that we were being watched made it more so. Without ropes or other climbing gear, we navigated the steep, slippery incline, assisting each other by grabbing rifles and rucksacks. At the top, at 50% alert, we settled in for the night.

The next day, June 17, we continued our mission. Soon after, we discovered a cache of 384 brand-new, swathed in cosmoline and covered in waxed paper, Chinese Type 56 7.62X39MM semi-automatic carbines with Spiker bayonet and adjustable iron sights. We cleared an LZ to take the rifles to FSB Myron. An NCO accompanied the rifles to ensure that each member of Dakota received a war trophy. He succeeded, and each Dakota soldier was rewarded with a rifle and the appropriate customs paperwork. My rifle sits in a gun case in my basement, in the same condition in which it was found.

On June 18, we stayed on the high ground and moved slowly and deliberately, occasionally dropping into the valley to recon. At the

105MM Howitzer, 2nd Battalion 40th Artillery, Somewhere in Cambodia 1970, Author's Collection

end of the day, we established an NDP and, at 50% alert, waited out the night.

Friday, June 19

Friday, June 19, was a pleasant day. With orders to continue our area sweep, we moved out, seeking additional cache locations in the vicinity of YU095-435. Dakota moved in a wedge formation: 1st Platoon in the center at the head of the wedge, again in the open following another well-worn track; 3rd Platoon and the command

PART 4 CAMBODIA MAY-JUNE 1970

element are on my right flank hugging the base of a small hill mass; 2nd Platoon was on my left flank weaving in and out of a tree line. Everyone was on high alert.

I walked point for 1st Platoon for the second day in a row. Everyone scanned the area and looked for threats, awaiting the explosion of a command-detonated anti-personnel mine with accompanying gunfire that signified an ambush. It seemed as if we were actors in a slow-motion movie.

My view of the trail and the area to the front was clear, and I could see the point men of the other platoons. Nothing seemed out of the ordinary. There appeared to be no indication of recent human activity, nor were there indications of booby traps. At approximately 1202 hours, we made contact with an enemy force of unknown size. The silence is shattered by an explosion to the right front of the formation. Bullets snapped the air around and over Dakota and ripped into the surrounding jungle. The roar of gunfire and explosions intensified as Dakota attempted fire superiority. Suddenly everything became extraordinarily clear to me, the broken branches falling; the dirt exploding as rounds struck the earth around us, the yells for ammo and medic, every minute movement. Dakota takes it all in instantaneously, comprehend it fully, even as we keep firing, reaching for a fresh magazine or belt of M-60 ammo, slamming them home and continuing to fire. There were yells and cursing, and a gut-felt terror grips soldiers with the realization that this was a well-placed ambush. We were in a fight for our lives.

My RTO, another soldier, and me were fully exposed at the front of the formation with no close cover. The crackling of the radio was barely heard over the sounds of combat. Grabbing the radio handset, I told the CO that the lead element of the 3rd Platoon was not returning fire and was presumed out of action. At the same time, I requested artillery and relayed the specifics to the company FO (forward observer). The battlespace to the front was obscured from direct observation by the CO and FO. I acted as their eyes. Soon artillery rounds fell on suspected enemy positions, and I adjusted as best I could.

Elements of the 3rd Platoon are pinned down by the heavy fire and cannot reach their fallen platoon mates. The 2nd Platoon is in no better position but can provide sustained fire on suspected enemy positions.

Firing slackens enough so that I can move toward the 3rd Platoon lead element and check the situation. Throwing smoke grenades to obscure our movement, a 1st Platoon soldier and I crawled out under sporadic but intense fire to the immobile soldiers. The three are observed to be KIA, probably from the blast of the command detonate explosive. We dragged two of them and an M-60 to a location close to the 1st Platoon. Throwing the last of the smoke grenades, I returned to retrieve the third fallen soldier.

An AH-1GS Cobra gunship hunter-killer team, the Blue Max of the 2nd Battalion 20th Artillery (Ariel Rocket Artillery), orbiting the battle, contacted me directly and offered assistance. The Cobra, firing 2.7-inch rockets, could bring fire to bear closer than field artillery. They are the logical choice for close-in support. After some negotiation because of the "danger close" impact zone, the gunships made several passes directing their 2.7-inch rockets into the enemy positions. Shortly afterward, the enemy stopped firing.

We continued to take sporadic harassing small arms fire throughout the rest of the day and into the night. The FO plotted H & I fire (Harassing and Interdiction) in an area 100 meters out and on all sides of the company positions. 100% alert waiting for the full-on attack. No one even thought of sleeping; adrenalin kept us awake and alert. An After Action Report of the 2nd Brigade 1st Cavalry Division reported that we killed 5 NVA. Doubtful.

Saturday, June 20

We cleared an LZ to remove the fallen (Michael William Notermann, Victoria, MN; Ronald Richard Stewart, Glenrock, WY; Johnny Mack Watson, Mobile, LA, all of the 3rd Platoon) and the wounded and to receive ammo and water. Almost immediately, a Huey hovered above it, and the crew chief kicked out the resupply.

PART 4 CAMBODIA MAY-JUNE 1970

Then the bird landed, and the battalion commander and the battalion command sergeant major (CSM) jumped out. The Huey departed for FSB Myron, and another replaced it orbiting above. The BN CO sought out the Dakota CO; the CSM mingled with the enlisted troops, offering comfort and encouragement while gathering first-person accounts of the action.

After twenty minutes with the Dakota CO, the BN CO approached me with the news that the Dakota CO was leaving and that the new CO, a captain, would arrive on the next bird. I was told not to screw things up and directed to move the company to the previous LZ and await the arrival of the new CO.

The orbiting Huey descended into the LZ. The passengers boarded. It lifted off. Immediately, it began taking machine-gun fire from a covered position on the hillside overlooking the LZ. There was shouting and cursing as the helicopter, taking hits, managed to lift off and head for FSB Myron. Our suppressing fire against the machine gun distracted the enemy and pissed them off. Dakota fought an on-again-off-again running gun battle for the next few hours as it moved to resecure the previous LZ. I hoped that we weren't walking into another and more devastating ambush.

We made it to the LZ without casualties, set up security, and awaited the new guy. The adrenalin began to wear off and the combat of the day and the previous day sunk in, the eyes of the Dakota soldiers reflected the relief at being alive and the guilt of surviving. The "1000-yard stare" was prevalent in others. But these guys, most draftees like myself, acted professionally and unselfishly. They had fought for and would again fight for each other.

An hour after our arrival at the LZ, a Huey landed and out stepped a figure clad in tiger-striped jungle fatigues, a bush hat of similar design, and a chip on his shoulder bigger than the state of Texas. On closer inspection, he had a 5th Special Forces patch on his right shoulder and carried, in addition to his M16A1, a foreign-made 9MM pistol with a silencer, a big combat knife attached to the front of his web gear, and a "blackjack" in his back trouser pocket. Was our new CO an ARVN (Army of the Republic of Vietnam) ranger? No. It turned out that he was just a short guy who forgot he was an American GI.

My first thought: "This a-hole is going to get us killed."

First impressions aren't that great. The CO's body language said it all: Dakota was a mess, undisciplined and lacking any semblance of a well-run infantry unit. His first action was to confiscate the CAR-15 one of my men carried. The soldier wasn't "authorized" to have it—the inference being that disciplinary action would follow, however, it never happened.

The CO moved Dakota approximately 50 meters up a hill and established an NDP on a narrow ridge. We heard the occasional squelch of enemy radios around the position.

As I walked the interior of the company positions, paying attention to the M-60 emplacements, I noticed the CO disappearing into the jungle below a 1st Platoon M-60 position. I asked the gunner if the CO said anything. "No," came the reply. Without a word, the CO just walked into the jungle. His movement, 15 to 25 meters below the Dakota positions, was heard. I followed him as he circled. And as I did, I informed each fighting position that the CO was reconnoitering; and to be careful before opening fire. Coming full circle, the CO began his ascent back to the perimeter. At a 2nd Platoon fighting position, the last on the perimeter, I cautioned the M-60 gunner to be alert. Just then, the CO emerged directly in front of the gun. Fortunately, disaster was averted; however, the CO wasn't pleased. It seemed that our noise discipline was lacking. He was equally guilty and that if it weren't for his noisy walk in the woods, I'd be looking at a dead man. It was an intense moment.

The CO gathered the two NCO acting platoon leaders and me for the operation order. At the time, we were a little more than 1500 meters from FSB Myron as the crow flies. The mission was to exfiltrate, by the most direct route to FSB Myron, initiating no contact with the enemy. Breathing a sigh of relief, the three of us returned to our platoons and passed the news. The news, short-lived though it would be, was welcomed, and morale lifted. This objective didn't include fighting and dying.

In retrospect, the difference between the two company COs was like night and day. The previous CO commanded respect, was steady, had a sense of humor, was calculating and aggressive when necessary. He didn't shy from a fight; he didn't get into one unnecessarily. The mission was critical; the soldiers under his command came first; he knew that there was no mission without them. His experience from his first tour informed his decisions. It prevented him from doing stupid things and carrying out ill-advised orders given from 500 feet above the jungle canopy or the relative safety of a firebase.

The new guy, in my opinion, was a cowboy in the worst sense: impulsive and overly aggressive. He was out of place in a straight-leg infantry unit. The chip on his shoulder and his perceptions about the company got in the way.

Sunday, June 21

After an uneventful night, we saddled up and moved out, the CO upfront, walking point. Occasionally we stopped to orient ourselves and to conduct close-in recon by the CO alone. Movement was slow going. Some in the 1st Platoon questioned why. The terrain was easy, and enemy activity was lacking. I speculated to myself that there was more to the mission than just getting to FSB Myron. After progressing about 300 meters, we stopped for the day and set up an NDP. Thankfully, this day was uneventful. The men of Dakota seemed relaxed; they remained vigilant.

Monday, June 22

Dawn broke, the sun filtered through the jungle canopy. Spirits ran high as a map recon indicated that Dakota would probably enter FSB Myron the next day. Rations were low, so breakfast was sparse—coffee and a "hockey puck" fruit cake for me.

With the CO again on point, Dakota moved in file: 2nd Platoon with the command element; then the depleted 3rd Platoon, with 1st Platoon bringing up the rear. By the end of the day, company strength would be fewer than sixty.

At the beginning of the Sanctuary Campaign, Dakota Company had a complement of 110, including three officers. On this day, Dakota had about sixty with two officers. I was the only officer remaining of the original three. If the force that we were against was supposedly significant, I wondered why understrength companies were sent into Cambodia.

Dakota angled to the left and descended into the valley and away from the safety of the ridge. A member of the command group relayed that an obstruction blocked the way and that the CO found a more accessible way around. A short time later, Dakota stood on another well-used trail. I was not surprised. I sensed that the CO was looking for his big score. I didn't know until years later that the BN CO thought that Dakota wasn't aggressive enough and that the action of June 19 proved it. The new guy intended to change that perception.

We pressed on a short distance into the suspected PAVN logistics area, one found the previous day by the BN CO during his visual air recon. The platoons leapfrogged down the trail, one platoon providing overwatch as another moved forward; the trailing platoon provided rear security. 1st Platoon stopped at the junction where a narrow trail branched from the main trail. The CO moved forward, took several soldiers from the 1st Platoon, and followed the side trail. Shortly, there was loud banging and other noises consistent with the destruction of a structure. Thankfully there was no gunfire. But the noise posed a problem: Even if the PAVN knew we were in their logistics encampment, the noise confirmed just how close.

The CO returned empty-handed but was happy that he destroyed some enemy property. That was when I showed him the five evenly spaced wires neatly placed along the right side of the trail. Two of those were strung across the tail, eventually leading to the previously discovered hootch. The other three continued straight, in parallel with the trail we were on. The pucker factor intensifies.

PART 4 CAMBODIA MAY-JUNE 1970

1st Platoon moved forward to a point where the trail bore to the left and out of sight. We took up positions as the 2nd Platoon passed through, the lead element disappeared from our line of sight. At 1537 hours in the vicinity of YU086-431, we make contact with another NVA force of unknown size. There is an explosion. The sound comes from the area of the 2nd Platoon. Then concentrated fire from small arms, automatic weapons, and RPGs (Rifle Propelled Grenades) rake the formation. The fire comes at us from every direction as if the enemy is inside of our tactical formation. We returned fire, hoping for an advantage, but it isn't easy to pick targets. Then the fire intensified. I'm now sure that the PAVN has our number. I felt that it was beginning to be the Vietnam version of Custer's Last Stand. Bullets ripped through the foliage and kicked up dirt close behind our feet. Dakota stayed together and returned fire. The CO radioed a SITREP (Situation Report) and called for fire. He spotted movement near a bunker at the head of the trail leading up from the one we were on. He told me to make a frontal assault and take out the bunker. It was suicide; he knew it. From his perspective, it made sense. Take the fight to the enemy. But that could be accomplished without a frontal assault. I'm reminded of the "school solution" to a problem for a tactical assault on a Vietnamese village during OCS. A frontal assault on a well-defended village was required when an attack on the minimally defended rear was the most appropriate course of action. As the student company commander, that was my solution. Now, in Cambodia, it appeared that I was again faced with a similar circumstance. I positioned an M-60 to provide suppressing fire while I looked for ways to outflank the non-firing bunker. Just as quickly as it started, the enemy firing stopped.

We waited. Nothing. We waited some more. Still nothing. We assessed casualties and ammunition status. There was movement from the 2nd Platoon position. The platoon was withdrawing to the hastily developing company perimeter. The soldiers were running and carrying their wounded as best they could. Their dead (Charles Castulo Cisneros, Cero, NM and Allen Eugene Oatney, Waterville, KS) were left on the field. At my feet was Raul DeJesus-Rosa, Juncos, Puerto Rico of the 1st Platoon. The three are left on the field.

According to the 2nd Brigade 1st Cavalry Division (Airmobile) SITREP, Dakota was credited with 6 NVA KIA. Again, doubtful.

Between June 16 and June 22, Dakota Company lost seven KIA and several wounded. The dead were seven of the 105 soldiers of the 5th Battalion 12th Infantry killed during its forty-six months in South Vietnam. Private DeJesus-Rosa, posthumously promoted to sergeant, was the only KIA from the 1st Platoon during my time as a platoon leader.

After consulting with the BN CO, Dakota's CO told us to leave the dead on the field. He said that we would go back and get them the next day. Now Dakota needed to find a defensible extraction point and clear an LZ. The company was finally leaving this hell hole.

We begin the withdrawal. I exchanged my M16A1 for a 2nd Platoon M-60 (the gunner was wounded). Two others, also armed with M-60's, formed the rear guard, spraying the area with machine-gun bursts as we backed down the tail. I looked to my right. There was an open grassy area that we had passed earlier. There were several recently occupied spider holes. It was the perfect ambush site. The enemy had us surrounded and pinned with no hope of support. They had the opportunity to annihilate an entire infantry company. Yet, they let us go.

We rendezvoused without further contact and cleared an LZ. We were unsure what was next. We knew that no one was shooting at us and that aside from the three KIA, there were no severe casualties.

The CO told us that the battalion ordered our withdrawal. He said that he, along with volunteers, was staying to retrieve the fallen the next day. I was instructed to accompany the remainder of the company to FSB Myron. As we left, gunships orbited the LZ. The stay-behind group settled in for a restless night and prepared for the next day's recovery mission.

The remnants of Dakota arrived at FSB Myron. As I recall, no one greeted us. We were eventually told where to drop our gear and get

PART 4 CAMBODIA MAY-JUNE 1970

chow. This time, neither the BN CO nor the CSM was interested in our well-being. From my point of view, the men of Dakota were beaten down and mentally and physically done. At this point, it wouldn't have mattered what the BN CO said.

On the morning of June 25, the remnants of Dakota Company boarded a CH-47 Chinook helicopter for transport to Song Be.

The Cambodia adventure ended. The forty-two days in Cambodia, I am sure, made a lasting impression on the soldiers of the 5th Battalion 12th Infantry, especially those of Dakota Company. That many of us survived is a testament to our training, fortitude, and belief in others. Dakota, being a resilient crew, soldiered on, ready for whatever came next. Preferably early release and a trip back to The World.

PART 5
SOUTH VIETNAM, AGAIN

This thing is not going to last forever, and the flaming ferris wheel will continue to spin without you.

Marcus Luttrell

FSB Dreamer

AFTER A WELL-DESERVED standdown at Camp Frenzell-Jones, the soldiers of Dakota shipped to FSB Dreamer (YT020-250, YT925-267) in Binh Tuy Province. The FSB served as a transition between combat operations and preparation for the standdown and inactivation of the 199th Infantry Brigade (Light). Soldiers were selected according to DEROS (Date Estimated Return from Overseas) to accompany the brigade's colors to Fort Benning, Georgia, where the brigade would be inactivated. Those with significant time remaining in-country were assigned to other units within South Vietnam.

The time between July and September was filled with nothing significant. Tanh Linh was not a hotbed of VC activity. The CO's presence was not much in evidence despite the observation by both he and the battalion commander in Cambodia that Dakota required a significant

PART 5 SOUTH VIETNAM, AGAIN

amount of work to return it to a functioning infantry company. As busy work, elements of the 1st Platoon train RF/PF (Regional Force/Popular Force) soldiers in marksmanship and conducted patrols close to FSB Dreamer. Before one such patrol, a 1st Platoon soldier refused a direct order to participate. He was restrained and removed pending disciplinary action. This was the only such incident in my time as platoon leader.

Later, while on this patrol, the 1st Platoon heard chopping sounds in the jungle below a ridgeline it was traversing. The area was not supposed to have civilians, so we waited, watched, and listened intensely to the activity. Unfortunately, there was no easy way to approach stealthily. I reported the situation and waited for instructions. Shortly, an accented voice comes on the radio and offered assistance. It was an Australian pilot in an OV-10 Bronco twin-turboprop light attack and observation aircraft. Its primary mission was forward air control. He offered to direct a few rounds into the area and said that he had access to 175MM cannon looking for a mission. I confirmed our coordinates and those of the suspected enemy activity. One round came in, and neither by sound nor observation landed anywhere near the target. Adjustment. Second shot. Explosion. Then the radio exploded with a string of obscenities. It seemed that the second round came too close to a gun Jeep team sitting at an intersection. Fortunately, there were no injuries. Simultaneously, the pilot and I realized too late that the fire adjustment used the observer target line rather than the gun target line as used for the 175MM cannon. Firing ceased. The pilot left the station, and the 1st Platoon continued on its original azimuth.

Tragedy strikes Dakota on a company operation when an overloaded and underpowered Huey crashes into the jungle while exiting a PZ. The Huey is destroyed, and the crew and soldiers of the 3rd Platoon, including the platoon leader, were seriously injured. The platoon leader had just returned, having been seconded to the 3rd Battalion 7th Infantry during the Cambodia operation.

73 Days and a Wake-up

In the home stretch, in 74 days, I'll be on a Freedom Flight headed for sunny southern California. It's September 14, 1970. The 199th Infantry Brigade (Light) is preparing to case the colors, and a lucky few will return to Fort Benning, Georgia, for the inactivation ceremony. The remaining unit members are reallocated to other units within South Vietnam. Even though I am favorably considered for an advisory position with the Military Assistance Command Vietnam (MACV), I received orders for the 23rd Infantry Division (AMERICAL) at Chu Lai. Chu Lai was located in I Corps and was a seaport area of Quang Nam Province. The US Marine Corps operated from Chu Lai between 1965 and 1970 when the base was turned over to the US Army. The 23rd Infantry Division (AMERICAL) operated out of a former USMC base on the Ky Ha peninsula from 1967 until 1971. Interestingly, Chu Lai is not a Vietnamese name. The story goes that it was the Mandarin characters for "Krulak," the name of the US Marine Corps Major General Victor Krulak, who named the area.

Assigned to the Americal Combat Center (Provisional) replacement company, I received my third "in-country" and unit orientation. After completing the week-long orientation, I reported to the assignments section of Division G-1. The assignment officer was a Captain and former member of the 199th Infantry Brigade (Light). After some reminiscing about the brigade and possible assignment to a unit operating in the "Rocket Pocket" (BS525-954), we agreed on an assignment as an Assistant G-1. My job: to manage the Division Officer Club System. This was much better than counting Butterfingers at the PX.

Round Eyes, The Courtesy Patrol, Boonie Hats, and Carling Black Label

In addition to ensuring that the O-Club system was operating per regulation and that each club received its allocation of food and

PART 5 SOUTH VIETNAM, AGAIN

beverages, I scheduled entertainment—mostly small local Vietnamese bands, covering US and British bands, and the occasional American touring band. The latter was much anticipated. The female singers in the Vietnamese bands are attractive, most having French features, but the American singers with their "round" eyes are reminders of home. This leads to some interesting situations.

The Division O-Club system headquarters, so to speak, was located in a compound just below the Division headquarters and the senior officer quarters. There was a business office, a warehouse, my office and quarters, enlisted staff quarters, showers, a kitchen with an outdoor grill, and accommodations for an American touring band. The NCO Club system was set up similarly.

One evening, around 2300 hours (11:00 PM), we returned from a gig at the 27th Surgical Hospital and prepared a cookout for the band. This is standard for all the US bands performing at O-Club venues in Chu Lai. This cookout was one of the more memorable ones. During the performance at the O-Club, a captain engaged one of the female performers in conversation. Innocent at first, it bordered on stalking by night's end. As we loaded up the band for the return to the compound, the captain insisted on taking his "friend" back to the compound in his Jeep. He explained that they knew each other in high school and had some catching up to do. Much to his chagrin, I told him "No," and we drove away. During the drive back to the compound, the entertainer confided that she did know this guy from high school and that he was then and is now a horse's ass. She wanted nothing to do with him.

We arrived at the compound. The captain followed us back and attempted to worm his way into the party. I told him "No." It was after curfew, the compound was off-limits, he needed to go to his quarters. He left.

On nights like this, we posted a guard at the entrance to repel unwanted guests. Not surprisingly, the guard told me that a captain wanted to enter. I approached the captain and reminded him of our previous conversation. Pissed, he left in his Jeep and drove up the hill. Knowing that this was not over, I relieved the guard of his M16A1 and assumed guard duty. I walked from the gate and slipped past the warehouse and took a hidden position to observe the road and the gate.

Lights out, the engine off, the Jeep sat on the road at the top of the hill. Eventually there is movement. A figure jumped into the Jeep, and the Jeep, transmission in neutral, proceeded downhill, gradually picking up speed. Occasionally brake lights flashed. The Jeep rolled to a stop just inside the gate. In silence, the three passengers sat and surveyed the area. Unbeknownst to them, I worked my way behind them and stood not more than ten feet behind the Jeep. It was deadly silent. Then, the silence was shattered by the sound of an M16A1 bolt slamming forward as I chambered the 5.56MM round—an attention-getter to those in the Jeep. I imagined their hearts jumping into their throats and maybe someone wetting themselves. As I approached, a shaking lieutenant exited the Jeep and said, "Do you know who this is?" "No. And frankly, it doesn't matter," I responded. "This area is off limits." The lieutenant proceeded to tell me that the captain was a general's aide. He must have thought that I'd be impressed. About this time, my NCOIC (non-commissioned officer in charge) approached as I told both the lieutenant and the captain that I didn't "give a rat's ass" who they worked for and that they should leave. I turned to the NCOIC and tell him to call the MPs (military police), at which point the lieutenant jumped in the Jeep and sped off.

The next morning I was told to report to the division chief of staff. "This should be fun," I thought. In my explanation, I provided details that the captain omitted in his complaint. The chief listened intently and chuckled when I told him about the bolt slamming forward. He reminded me that my actions were not something done in garrison and that I should work on a more tactful approach. I sensed that this was the extent of the reprimand. The chief's tone indicated that the captain was a pain in the ass and had done similar things in the past.

Chu Lai was a garrison town and the 23rd Infantry Division Post seemed to contain all of the worst aspects of garrisons in the US

PART 5 SOUTH VIETNAM, AGAIN

Especially the BS. One feature was the "courtesy" patrol. There was, in my opinion, nothing courteous about this patrol. NCOs, with no other job, patrol in pairs looking for any and every uniform violation that they can find. The most egregious violation was wearing the Boonie hat instead of the mandated baseball-style hat. I wore my Boonie hat like a badge of honor and was called on it many times, but nothing serious ever happened.

One day, outside the main PX, I spotted two soldiers in a heated one-sided conversation with the courtesy patrol. Their infraction? Not looking like garrison soldiers. These soldiers just returned from the field. They were dirty, unshaven, had combat gear, less a weapon, and were wearing the infamous Boonie hat. The Catch-22: the soldiers needed toiletries to clean up, but they couldn't get them from the PX until they cleaned up and looked like garrison soldiers. Their tour in Vietnam was completed; the soldiers came directly from the field and were headed to the replacement company for out-processing and return to state-side. The NCOs, both with CIBs, forgot where they came from. Rather than finding a way to help the soldiers, the NCOs were bureaucrats without common sense, enforcing regulations to the letter of the law. No compromise. After observing the exchange, I offered to help.

Upon returning to the office, I was told the chief of staff wanted to see me. News travels fast. Another counseling session and an admonition to trim my sideburns and mustache. The chief said nothing about my Boonie hat.

On another occasion, I received a call from our warehouse sergeant. He was at the main supply depot and was told that he had to take two pallets of Carling Black Label beer instead of the regular two pallets of Budweiser. "No Black Label, no beer." I talked with the depot NCO and negotiated to take one pallet of each. Now Carling was bad enough, but when it had been sitting in a depot, first in Saigon and then in Chu Lai, it did not age well. I was now faced with the problem of unloading the unsavory beer. Me, the NCOIC, and the office staff brainstormed ideas. Nothing. I finally directed that the clubs receive only the Carling and that they get the Budweiser when the Carling was sold out. Much pushback. Recalling my field experience, I believed that the officers would drink anything put before them. Wrong. Garrison officers were very picky. The beer didn't move. Liquor sales increased, though.

After the fact, the supply sergeant told me that he tried to make a deal with the Vietnamese, but they didn't want the Carling. Unable to sell, give away, or return the Carling to the main warehouse, we wrote the Carling off as spoiled goods and took it to the dump. Speaking of the dump, on Thanksgiving 1970, the Chu Lai dump posted a sign with the words THIS DUMP CLOSED ON THANKSGIVING. Arlo Guthrie's song "Alice's Restaurant" came to mind.

Chu Lai, South Vietnam, "This Dump Closed on Thanksgiving," 1970, Author's Collection

PART 6
THE WORLD – 1971

Such is the patriot's boast, where'er we roam/His first, best country ever is, at home.

Oliver Goldsmith

HOME

IN LATE NOVEMBER 1970, I returned to "The World," a term used to describe any place not South Vietnam but specifically the United States. The long flight was anticlimactic. I was happy to leave, but I was drawn to the idea of returning to Vietnam after a break. There was unfinished business. More importantly, I missed the action and the challenges.

The homecoming was not what I expected. No crowds, no greetings. As I walked in uniform through the terminal at LAX, my duffel bag and war trophy in hand, I was met with indifference. Fortunately, there was not the anti-war reception that I was told to expect. Once home, I settled in for a short leave. My hair, mustache, and sideburns were a little longer, and I didn't wear a uniform in public, especially in California, and I didn't talk about the war. Strangers "knew" that I was a soldier and probably an officer. It's not something easy to disguise. I couldn't wait to return to Fort Ord and the comfort of being surrounded by people in uniform.

Fort Ord

Fort Ord was located on the Monterey Peninsula, six miles east of Monterey, approximately 340 miles north of Los Angeles, and 80 miles south of San Francisco. The fort was established in 1917 as Camp Gigling to train infantry troops. In 1933, War Department General Order 11 designated Camp Gigling Camp Ord to honor Major General O. E. Ord, a Civil War Commander of Union Troops, West Point Class of 1839. In 1940, Fort Ord, previously Camp Ord, was commanded by Brigadier General Joseph "Vinegar Joe" Stilwell, who also commanded the 7th Infantry Division. After training as a Motorized Division in the Mohave Desert, the Division returned to Fort Ord for amphibious training in preparation for deployment, in 1943, to expel the Japanese from the Aleutian Islands of Alaska.

During World War II, famous fighting Divisions (3rd, 27th, 43rd and 5th) were also deployed from Fort Ord. The fort served as a basic combat infantry training center between 1947 and 1975. And during the 1960s, it was a staging area for units deploying to Southeast Asia. In 1975, unit training ended, and the 7th Infantry Division returned, where it remained until the early 1990s. During its active service, Fort Ord trained as many as 1.5 million troops. Fort Ord was inactivated in 1994, ending a chapter rich in US Army history. Today 14,651 acres of the original 44-square-mile installation is the Fort Ord National Monument, established by proclamation on April 20, 2012.

Between January 1971 and April 1972, I was stationed at Fort Ord. The cantonment area and the lush savannah, gnarled scrub oaks, rugged hills bordering shrub-lined canyons hadn't changed since my departure in 1969. Even though we went about the business of war, it was peaceful and welcoming. I was assigned as an Assistant S-3 (Operations and Training) with the Training Command (Provisional) of the US Army Training center (USATC). In April 1971, as a newly promoted captain, I was reassigned to the Small Arms and Recoilless Rifle Subcommittee as chief. I was responsible for the operation of most of the inland ranges and the training conducted on them: training on the M203 and M-79 grenade launchers, the M60 and .50-caliber M2 machine guns, the 90MM recoilless rifle, the M72A2 light anti-tank weapon, hand grenades, and the .45-caliber pistol, among other things—all weapons that I used or had familiarity with while in Vietnam.

My boss was a major. When I met him, I noticed the nameplate on his desk with the inscription MAJOR SPIGGS. The name wasn't real. I listened as he explained my duties and responsibilities, but my eyes were focused on the nameplate. He stopped and, with a chuckle, told me that SPIGGS meant "Self-Paced and Integrated Goat Screw," which is what he said that he oversaw regarding the training and range operations. It was the end of the duty day, so the major suggested that we continue the "orientation" at the O-Club. We, along with other officers, headed to Parker Flats and the casual bar. It was a very interesting Friday night.

My routine, one that I kept up during my time as committee chief, was to go to a range at first light to oversee the delivery, inventory, and acceptance of ammunition, followed by breakfast at the golf course (Fort Ord had two co-located courses, Bayonet and Black Horse, both PGA-level courses occasionally used for practice during Pebble Beach tournaments) and then a visit to the committee office and storage facility on the main post. Then back to the ranges, lunch at the O-Club or the golf course, and back to the ranges again. I practically lived on mass quantities of Coca-Cola and black Army coffee. I spent most nights at the O-Club (casual bar) or in Monterey, Carmel, or Salinas hanging out with other Vietnam veterans or those who just missed assignments to South Vietnam. We talked a lot about how things were, are currently, and would be in the future. The more talking there was, the less isolated I felt, and the more accepting of my role as an infantry officer in Vietnam and Cambodia.

Range 48 was a fun range to operate. It was where we held the monthly weapons demonstration, demonstrating how each crew-served weapon was integrated with and supported an infantry rifle squad in the defense. The highlight was the "mad minute" at the end of the attack. We chose a squad of soldiers from an AIT company to occupy fighting positions in front of the bleachers. The bleachers contained visiting dignitaries and AIT students about to graduate. From the range tower, a lieutenant, in a somber tone, introduced the scenario: an enemy force approaching the fighting positions to the front. Each crew-served weapon was brought to bear on the "advancing enemy." First the mortars, then the .50-caliber M2 machine guns, then the M60 machine guns. A 90MM and M72A2 LAW engaged stationary armor vehicles at the left and right limits. Finally, a smoke grenade signaled the fighting positions to unleash hell on the close-in advancing enemy. The end. Applause. During one of our discussions on improving the experience, several NCOs and I thought that it would be more realistic if we fired over or into the bleachers. Fortunately for the dignitaries and soldiers in those bleachers, we were joking.

Hanoi Jane

Fort Ord, along with Fort MacArthur in the Los Angeles area and especially Oakland Army Base in proximity to UC Berkeley in the San Francisco Bay area, was a focal point for the Vietnam anti-war movement in California. One day the protests and demonstrations arrived at Fort Ord. Earlier, we got word of demonstrations planned for the front gate area. The Training Command (Provisional) was tasked to provide senior NCOs to support the MPs, specifically manning an observation post on the roof of the post-movie theater, to provide updates on the demonstrator's movements. There was a rumor that Jane (soon to be "Hanoi Jane") Fonda would be amongst the protestors. Several of the NCOs, Vietnam combat veterans all, requested sniper rifles and authorization to "take out the enemy" at the appropriate time. The MPs, concerned that one of the NCOs would bring his own rifle, provided an officer to ensure that it didn't happen. As I recall, the demonstration was a dud, I don't recall if Fonda even showed up. Eventually, the demonstrators moved to their next demonstration target. No demonstrators were hurt.

Life After Active Duty

In April 1972, I was released from active duty—one of the many officers in the grade of captain and major cut from the Army rolls during the reduction in force of that year. I entered the US Army Reserve and served in transportation, training, and garrison units in the San Francisco Bay area. In 1985 I escaped from California for a civilian job with the Department of the Army at Fort Belvoir, Virginia. I served in the Army National Guard in transportation, mobilization, and operations. I returned to the US Army Reserve in 1991, where I commanded a multi-service military police detachment and then served as an Individual Mobilization Augmentee. I transferred to the Retired Reserve in 1997.

In slightly less than thirty years in uniform, I served in all three components of the US Army. Not a day goes by when I don't think about those with whom I served. Especially those soldiers of Dakota Company 5th Battalion 12th Infantry 199th Infantry Brigade (Light).

EPILOGUE

The Draft

BETWEEN 1964 (THE beginning of the Peacetime Draft) and 1973 (the end of the Peacetime Draft), "conscription" and "draft" were nasty words. They were a catalyst and rallying cry for the anti-war and draft-resistance movements in the United States. Writings of the time portrayed the draft as evil and despicable, focusing on those considered privileged; the "Fortunate Sons," the ones who manipulated the system to avoid the draft. Two future presidents and one future vice president, among others, were in that group.

The draft was often seen as a racial issue, focusing on societal disgust regarding a specific group within the Armed Forces. In writings, alleged disparities between minority and non-minority groups were "backed up" by statistics, some of dubious nature and interpretation. Discussions focused on the percentages of this or that group; ratios of killed and wounded of one particular group; ratios of population participation—meaningless in the grand scheme of things but serving the political propaganda purpose at the time. Missing, then as now, is any mention of the valor of those in that group. Those who fought well for and with their brothers in arms. Who made the same sacrifices, or perhaps more significant sacrifices, as those who fought side-by-side. Today, it seems that nothing has changed, as racial politics has seeped into every aspect of our society and the Armed Forces.

EPILOGUE

Project (McNamara's) 100,000

Within the category of draftee was a group called Project 100,000. During the Vietnam War, over 500,000 draftees were part of the Project. Think of it. Out of a draftee pool of 1,875,304, 27% were Project 100,000. Why is this significant? Because it was a social experiment, a part of the "War on Poverty," from the brain of then-Secretary of Defense, Robert McNamara. A project designed to raise (allegedly) participants out of poverty and meet escalating manpower requirements in Vietnam.

McNamara, the consummate techno-nerd, was convinced that technology and computers would win the war. Specifically, he thought—no, he was convinced—that videotapes were the key to raising intelligence. McNamara thought his program would make productive citizens. The project was a disaster. In effect, he created cannon fodder.

The people in the project were of low IQ, mostly illiterate with barely a third-grade reading level. The pool of draftees in the program included a few officers (through OCS) and a large enlisted cohort. Both were untrainable and placed a significant burden on the units to which assigned. Dakota Company 5th Battalion 12th Infantry 199th Brigade (Light) had two "soldiers," an officer and enlisted. The officer, who on the surface appeared squared away, lasted maybe two weeks. He left the company after his first firefight in Cambodia. His ultimate fate is unknown. Hopefully, he was sent back to the States and released from active duty. The enlisted "soldier" was so incompetent and untrustworthy that he wasn't allowed to carry a weapon of any kind. He did carry a radio antenna called a two-niner-two (292). The antenna, used by the company command element, was a VHF low band ¼ wave vertical antenna designed to work in the jungle. Many times he climbed a tree to get the best possible reception. The "soldier" went AWOL in Cambodia and eventually attempted to board a Freedom Flight from Da Nang. He was arrested and charged with numerous counts that landed him in the disciplinary barracks at Fort Leavenworth, Kansas. After the war, remnants of this program remained. A US Army Reserve transportation battalion I served in had one.

The All-Volunteer Force

Another consequence (positive in my view) of the Vietnam War was the All-Volunteer Military. It was a reaction to the draft and the draft's real and perceived inequities. Since its inception, the Armed Forces have seen a rise in professionalism in the enlisted ranks and better-trained officers. Better equipped and trained, soldiers, sailors, airmen, Marines, and the Coast Guard have supported and defended (and sacrificed for) the Constitution of the United States against foreign enemies, especially since September 11, 2001. Despite this, the program is a target of opportunity for a contingent of the disaffected and delusional who hate the military and seek to diminish it, to the peril of the United States. They hate the military for an alleged lack of "diversity" and "inclusiveness." They tell us that diversity and inclusiveness enhance the effectiveness of combat and combat support units. Yet, they don't explain why and how, because they can't. They also argue that an All-Volunteer Military perpetuates the notion of privilege. Examples given are cherry-picked or made up from whole cloth to give the allusion of widespread lack of both. Everything is questioned in our politically correct environment, and individuals and institutions are denigrated. And more than ever, the military is being used as a platform for social engineering.

The politicians are no better. Afraid of their own shadow, they manipulate the defense budget to satisfy a small base of constituents and for self-aggrandizement, and perhaps self-enrichment, cutting programs beneficial to the defense of the United States to move money into a social agenda of a dubious nature, spending taxpayer money on services and procedures to serve a tiny population while using the service or procedure as an enticement to join the Armed Forces.

The voting public needs to wise up. Otherwise, a military that has

EPILOGUE

protected our freedoms since the nation's founding will be as hollow or even more hollow than it was in the 1970s.

That being said, there are intangible benefits to serving in today's military. There is the satisfaction of belonging to something larger than oneself, of being a member of a team that, in many ways, is like a family. And being a part of the world's best-trained and -equipped military.

AFTERWORD

"It was my pleasure."

WHEN SOMEONE THANKS me for my service, I respond, "It was my pleasure," followed by "It was down payment on a debt owed." My service is a debt that I cannot repay. It is a debt that I owe to those soldiers, sailors, airmen and Marines who came before me, especially the 58,220 heroes whose names are engraved on the Vietnam Memorial. Thus, the down payment.

I also owe a debt to my father and his five brothers and my mother's two brothers who served in World War II in the Navy, Army, Army Air Corps, and as a civilian contractor. Especially the two who were prisoners of war in different theaters.

In 1941, Aloysius (Al) Ambrose, age twenty-six, was a civilian working with the US Navy Bureau of Yards and Docks on Wake Island in the Pacific. Simultaneously with the attack on Pearl Harbor, the Japanese began a continuous bombardment of Wake Island, preparing for a ground assault. On December 28, the garrison surrendered. Ninety Americans, primarily civilian contractors, were taken off the island and shipped to Japan. Al was one of them. These prisoners were the lucky ones. When the Japanese abandoned the island in 1945, those remaining prisoners were summarily executed.

Records indicate that the Japanese took Al and the others to Osaka Main Camp Chikko Osaka 34-135. The prisoners were used to

AFTERWORD

load and offload ships and maintain the port facilities. The US Army Air Corps bombed the Osaka Main Camp on numerous occasions, necessitating prisoners moving at least twice. Some reports put the prisoners in Shanghai, China.

On June 6, 1944, nineteen-year-old Victor Edward (Vic) jumped into Normandy in the early-morning hours. Victor was a paratrooper assigned to E Company, 507th Parachute Infantry Regiment, a "nondivisional" unit of the 82nd Division (Airborne). Victor was wounded and captured by the Germans. On June 20, he entered a German surgical hospital where his left hand was amputated. Upon release on July 12, he was relocated to Stalag 7, Moosburg, Germany, in the German state of Bavaria, where he spent the remainder of the war. Victor was medically discharged as a sergeant and was awarded the Purple Heart.

Both Al and Victor were repatriated in September 1945.

My father, John Stephen (John), enlisted in the US Navy in 1940. He had his first Christmas away from home aboard the USS *Nashville* (CL-43), where he served from 1940 to 1946 as a fire control technician and as Senior Chief of Division F by the end of the war. He was awarded the Bronze Star with Combat "V." The *Nashville* was a Brooklyn class light cruiser. The *Nashville* escorted the carrier USS *Hornet* with sixteen B-25 bombers for what became known as the Doolittle Raid on Japan on April 18, 1942. The *Nashville* provided fire support for numerous operations, shelling targets in New Guinea, the Admiralty Islands, Bougainville, and Cape Gloucester, New Britain, to name a few. The *Nashville* carried General Douglas MacArthur on three occasions, the final time to Leyte, in the Philippines, when he returned. On December 13, 1944, the *Nashville* was struck by a kamikaze, killing 133 and wounding 190. The *Nashville* received ten Battle Stars during World War II. John made the Navy a career, retiring in 1963.

John's brother Cyril (Cy) served aboard the USS Atlas (ARL-7), *ARL* standing for Auxiliary Repair Ship Light, an Achelous-class landing craft repair ship. Ships of this class repaired damaged landing craft. The *Atlas* arrived off of the Normandy beaches on June 8 and began repairing damaged landing craft. The *Atlas* received one Battle Star during World War II. Cy made a twenty-year career in the Navy, retiring as Engineman First Class. He was a certified salvage diver.

Two brothers served in the US Army Air Corps. Stephen Jr. (Steve) was drafted on April 8, 1942, and eventually assigned to Waco Army Air Field in Waco, Texas, a training center for basic military skills and tactical flying. In 1942, the airfield was part of the Gulf Coast Training Center of the Central Flying Training Command. Stephen was a staff sergeant. Daniel (Dan) Francis served from 1942 to 1945. He worked in ordnance, probably with the 8th or 9th Air Force in England and France. He was a private first class.

My mother had two brothers who served in the Pacific Theater. Joseph (Joe) was in the Navy. He was a machine gunner on a TBM (Avenger) aircraft flying from the USS *Monterey* (CVL-26) and USS *Belleau Wood* (CVL-24). His Aviator's Flight Log Book indicates that he was one lucky guy. Ellsworth (Els) was a US Army medic with the 7th Infantry Division. Both returned to civilian life after the war.

In Memory

The Vietnam Memorial in Washington D.C. Panel 9W contains the names of those soldiers assigned and attached to Dakota Company who were killed in action in Cambodia in June 1970. May they rest in Peace. Tuesday, June 16: Frederick Richard Levins, Naples, FL, 76th Infantry Platoon Combat Tracker (L57). Friday, June 19: Michael William Notermann, Victoria, MN (L69), 3rd Platoon; Ronald Richard Stewart, Glenrock, WY (L70), 3rd Platoon; Johnny Mack Watson, Mobile, AL (L71), 3rd Platoon. Monday, June 22: Charles Castulo Cisneros, Cero, NM (L78), 2nd Platoon; Allen Eugene Oatney, Waterville, KS (L78), 2nd Platoon; Raul DeJesus-Rosa, Juncos, Puerto Rico (L78), 1st Platoon.

ACKNOWLEDGMENTS

THE COVER OF this book is a work of digital artistry. Chase Nickoles, a very talented young artist, took a back-of-the-envelope concept and interpreted it beautifully. Many thanks. Thank you, Bob Shellhammer, for your masterful restoration of my fifty-year-old photographs. Thank you, Lyndi McNulty and James Voter, for wading through drafts of the book and for providing suggestions and insights for improvement. Thank you, Joseph Michaels. Your interest in the Vietnam War and your thoughtful questions and those of your family helped me to frame the story.

CPSIA information can be obtained
at www.ICGtesting.com
Printed in the USA
BVHW031319130423
662297BV00020B/113